Mom's Cooking & More

Indian Style

(Indian Cuisine and Culture)

Dr. Anila Bali

Published by **Bali** Publications

Mom's Cooking & More *Indian Style*

ISBN 978-0-9559570-0-0

Published by **Bali** Publications
4 The Willows,
Old Park Road,
Ballymena
BT42 1QN
N.Ireland

Printed and bound in Great Britain by
Graham & Heslip Printers Ltd.
Alanbrooke Road,
Belfast
BT6 9HF

1st Printed in the UK in July 2008
Reprinted in January 2009

Foreword

This is a personal book. It is not an encyclopaedia of facts or a mine of information . It is an expression of my childhood memories interspersed with my mother's and grandmothers' cooking, recipes, tips and advice and later teaching my friends, particularly in Northern Ireland, the same. In between the two was the time period when I practised those dishes and their variations on my family; husband and twin sons who were always my food tasters! The ones they really liked became my party dishes for my friends who wanted to learn this home food which was not greasy and whose spices, particularly the chilli element, could be regulated to their taste. Being a lecturer by profession as I taught history, this was a challenge I enjoyed so I wrote the recipes for my friends, answered their questions, and told them about the practical uses of the spices and my childhood memories of learning about them. Twenty years later when I realized that these same friends were still cooking from the same recipes I decided to compile them together. I had, of course, held a lot more classes and given demonstrations in various women's institutes, mothers unions and rotary clubs where these got inter linked with cultural issues of India; the significance of Bindis and Bangles; the story of Divaali; how is a sari draped; hence the inclusion of these and more in this book.

This is not a perfect book with perfect recipes. It is a book of home cooked wholesome food, easy to make, cost effective and time efficient. I have included variations and steps in some of the recipes to convert them into party dishes with minimum effort.

The basis of this book is the dishes it incorporates; for this I would like to appreciate my twin sons Sanjeev and Anish who, from a very early age, tasted everything I made; gave their honest opinions, generally liked most things and encouraged me at every step to keep moving forward. It would be incomplete without a mention of our friend Jim Dempsey, who spent many an afternoon photographing the dishes that I would have cooked in the morning. The pictures have been excellent; many thanks to him. I have a group of friends without whom I could not have arrived at this stage; the ones who have always appreciated my cooking, wanted the recipes, even wanted me to open a restaurant; and those who have read my early manuscripts and offered their suggestions. I would also like to express my appreciation to my printers Graham and Heslip Ltd, especially to Colin Moffatt for coordinating the printing with efficient time management and to Annette Nugent for the vibrant designs and layout. Last but not the least, my husband, Indermohan, who has always loved my cooking, has been my total support in encouraging me in this venture. He has photographed, proof read, edited and taken over when I have been too tired to do anymore. Without him, his suggestions and eye for detail I could not have arrived at this stage.

I hope my readers will enjoy reading and learning these recipes as much as I have done writing them.

Dr Anila Bali
PhD. in History

left to right:
Wilma Bloomer, Ann Elkin, Betty Agarwala, Anila Bali, Nadine Bain, Alison Black, Rosemary Wilson

Mom Knows Best

Anila's decision to hold classes on Indian cuisine, in the early eighties timed very well with a general desire to try new things, an increased availability of new unfamiliar ingredients in the shops and Madhur Jaffrey's Indian cookery programmes on television. Since there were few Indian takeaways and even fewer restaurants in Northern Ireland it was great to learn how to reproduce a good range of authentic Indian dishes at home which were neither greasy nor too hot for our palettes. Anila taught us about the different spices and how to mix and match them, we asked, she answered and demonstrated by making the dishes in front of us. To encourage us to experiment with Indian cooking she gave us a starter pack of spices, basmati rice and chapathi flour as such ingredients were unknown and generally not easily available. Then came the good part; we got to eat what she had prepared. Her enthusiasm and anecdotes made our cooking mornings enjoyable. Since then we have been entertained many a time in her house; always with Indian dishes, old and new but interesting, spicy and full of zest.

Food and friendship, a winning combination.

Today, even with the supermarkets bringing in a choice of "Indian dishes" our families, children and now the daughters-in-law and sons-in-law, are still cooking from those twenty five year old recipes and would definitely prefer those dishes to the commercial varieties of today.

Wilma Bloomer

Ann Elliott

Betty Agarwal

Ladmie Pain

Alison Black

Rosemary Wilson

Contents

Introduction & Spices

When I first came to Northern Ireland in l972, with twin sons three years old, for a term of two years so that my husband could do his Ph.D. in Anaesthetics in the Royal Victoria Hospital, I was young, naive and inexperienced. I expected the whole world to be like my street in Delhi where I could walk down to the shops, pick up my daily requirements, come home, organise and cook for the day. When I walked down Lisburn Road, I quickly realized two things: - *firstly;* I could not get Indian spices, Indian vegetables or fruits - even meat the way I wanted, off the racks or in the shops. *Secondly;* I would have to be inquisitive and innovative, which I was, but even this got me nowhere.

Indian food at this time was not in vogue in Northern Ireland. Not only were the ingredients unavailable, there were no Indian restaurants, shops or take-aways. The Irish did not quite know what spicy food was all about. In fact, even if I had my husband's colleagues over for a meal, I quickly learned to make what I called a "safe dish" which was eggs and vegetables, baked in a white sauce. It always came in useful. However, when I came back to live here on a permanent basis in l980, I noticed a distinct change. Health food shops and later supermarkets had started to experiment with the better known spices like turmeric and red chillies, a few pickles, lentils, even kidney beans and chickpeas. Aubergines, red and green peppers, sweet potatoes, okras, garlic, ginger and coriander started to make their way into the green grocers, and girls started to observe these different vegetables and spices with curiosity. Colleagues who came over for dinner to our place showed keen interest in the spicy food and my "safe dish" started to go untouched.

Recipes started to be written, discussions held, whys and wherefores clarified and soon I was giving Indian cookery lessons to my friends at organised times, once a week, for ten weeks, just so they would not come knocking at my door at any and all times wanting recipes of dishes they had eaten in my house the previous day or week, or a clarification of those that may have been on television in Madhur Jaffrey's programme, or a discussion on their latest Indian cookery book they may have picked up.

Over the last 26 years I have seen interest in Indian food on a constant upward swing, possibly for three reasons:- *firstly;* easier global travel in the 80s and 90s means more people are exposed to different foreign foods; *secondly;* there is now a tendency to reduce the intake of meat in the daily diet and Indian food is well known for its vegetarian appeal; *thirdly;* Indian food also has vast scope to cope with all palates, from the hot to the mild, yet making the food interesting and spicy.

So, what is Indian food?

Is it the hot chilli food, traditionally talked about as that which would bring sweat and tears when eating it; or this spicy food with an Eastern promise, which is catching on the imagination of more and more people, so much so that it is now appearing on the shelves of chain stores like Sainsbury, Tesco, and Marks & Spencer in pre-packed meals, and the addition of a new dish with a regularity that I have not seen in any other food line for a long time.

But first I must clarify the point, that the term *'curry'*, which in the west signifies any Indian dish, is not an Indian term. It seems to be a word that came into usage during the British Raj days and has just crept into an everyday vocabulary. In Indian food there is a dish called *'Karhi'* which is an unusual, vegetarian Panjabi and Rajasthani dish, made with gram flour dumplings in a yoghurt sauce. Once, again this was in 1972 when Indian restaurants or take-aways were non-existent, my husband invited an Indian friend to eat with us as I had made Karhi and rice for dinner, which of course more than delighted our friend. Five minutes later he was on the phone again to clarify whether we had meant just an ordinary 'curry', or did he hear it right as 'karhi'. To carry the point a bit further; today curry generally means a dish with a sauce in it, not just spices, in which case it is a dry spicy dish.

There are myths surrounding Indian food; Myth no. 1; that it takes a long evening to put together an Indian meal. I make Indian food every evening and it takes me no more than one hour to one hour and fifteen minutes from the time I open the fridge to the time that I serve food on the table and that includes making chapaathis or the Indian bread along with the curries. **Myth no. 2;** that Indian food cannot be cooked without our different shaped pans and dishes like **'Baltis', 'Karaahis'** and cast-iron griddles called 'Tavas'. When I first came here to Northern Ireland with two suitcases of clothes in 1972, I had twin boys three years old who were always hungry, a busy husband whom I only saw in the evenings, a very tight budget to work in, not one spice on the shelves, and very limited kitchen equipment in my rented accommodation. One visit to the Indian shop called 'Willow Park' in the city centre to collect Indian groceries and pickles and I was set to make curries every night.

Myth no. three; that Indian food is always hot, pungent and eye watering. It is spicy, not necessarily hot, as the style and panache of this food is the delicacy of heat according to the required taste and dish, and it can be easily regulated. There are six main ground spices used in our curries of which only one is actually hot, that is red chillies, which can be reduced in quantity or even substituted for paprika to give the look but not the heat. So much for myths.

But there are some **definitive points** in our food. **Firstly;** it puts **more emphasis on the cooking of the**

food than on the decorating of it.
Probably because it comes from a
land where the skill is practised by
uneducated chefs who have learnt
the art through years of apprenticeships
in traditional and conservative environments
where the need is basically for food. Therefore
their skill is devoted chiefly to that end than for
visual effects. These are now coming up more
in modern restaurants for the new city life style.
Secondly; there is **more emphasis on savouries rather
than sweets** in an Indian meal. It was a total surprise for me
in the initial years to go for a full course meal or a buffet, and
see a spread of 5-7 sweet on the side table. With us it would
be traditionally one, maybe two sweets for the desert. To
go to the extent of three would be over indulgence. This is
not to say we do not have sweetmeats. We do. They would
be something like pastries, with a large variation, but they are
more for tea time consumption and are collectively known as
'Mithai'. **Thirdly;** despite the hot climate of the country **there
is no such thing as either a salad meal or a cold meal** in
the Indian food culture. It is always hot. Sandwiches are for
teatime, or as a snack, never a meal. **Fourthly;** lamb is more
popular, chicken is the more expensive of the meats and fish is
very widely eaten as the variety has an enormous range from
the cheap to the very expensive. Pork is not very well received
mainly because there have been health reasons associated with
it and beef is sold sparingly, and in very limited delicatessens
only, chiefly for foreigners, as the cow has been a protected
animal of the country and was forbidden to be used for
culinary purposes.

Three more points to note; for the first; generally,
soups are not part of a traditional Indian meal. It has been
adapted to suit changing trends, but is still served only in the
winter
and then also in a casual
manner, more often than not steaming hot in soup mugs
during cocktails; not for a formal dinner. For the second, an
Indian meal is not served as individual meals either as starters
or main courses. The curried dishes are laid out in the centre
of the table from which everybody helps themselves, starters
having been passed around in platters as hors de oeuvre
with drinks. Generally, in a home an every day meal would
consist of one curry dish, be it vegetable or meat, or a lentil
or chickpeas or kidney beans; and one dry vegetable dish;
accompanied by yoghurt, salad and Indian bread or rice. For
more elaborate meals of course you can have as many dishes
in the centre of the table; a meat curry, a chicken, possibly even
a fish, lentils and vegetables. For the third point; for drinks,
it was traditional to have water, orange or buttermilk, called

'Lassi', but now wine, red and white, or beer, are being served, and being well liked. India has been the heart of vegetarianism as it has more of a vegetarian population, whether by choice or tradition, than anywhere else in the world. I have half relatives who do not eat any meat or fish at all. I have a mother, grandmother, aunts and uncles who do not even eat eggs. The rest of us who do eat meat, do not do so everyday. Maybe two or three evenings a week, and not even that in the summer months. Therefore we have excellent dishes in vegetables, lentils, rice, even cheese called 'Paneer', which is made indigenously and is the only cheese that I know of which can be curried without melting. This aspect of Indian cooking has generated a lot of interest in many of my friends here as they would like to cut down the intake of meat in their daily diet, but do not know how to make vegetables interesting as main dishes. A point to note here is that India's vegetarianism stems from religion and a way of life, not the modern healthy eating reasons. **Therefore our vegetarian dishes must be actually vegetarian, not just seen to be so.** Rice dishes, lentil, vegetable curries are all cooked with water, never stock, a fact which took me a long time to understand or come to terms with in the western cooking.

Here it must be noted that India is by and large vegetarian not vegan. Diet is supplemented chiefly and carefully with butter, cheese, milk and milk products. There are some religious sects like Jains who do not eat onion or garlic, but that is a very small number of people.

Till recently frozen food industry in India was non-existent. Even now it is neither easily available, nor financially possible. It is not even in much demand as there is a shortage of electricity in most parts of the country. Therefore in India, **cooking is woven round seasonal produce** which is abundant in the winter months; peas, carrots, cauliflower, turnip, spinach, apples, bananas, oranges; these being the favourites. In the summer months root vegetables are the norm, meat is too rich for the climate, and that is why possibly we are so dependent on the dried lentils, peas and beans for the main dishes.

An interesting point is that in India the **consumer milk is buffalo milk which is quite different to cow's milk.** It is richer milk; has a stronger taste; and the butter from it is white and fluffy in texture, which is different to the cow's butter which apart from being yellow has a much more firmer and buttery taste. Although pasteurisation has come in some of the big cities, milk in India is always boiled, left in a cool place for a few hours, so that a thick layer of cream forms on the top. This layer called 'Malai' is scooped out, the milk becomes virtually fat free, and the malai is used for baking, cooking, making butter and ghee or used in sweet dishes. Children love to spread it on top of toast and sprinkle sugar on it and have it any time of the day or night.

Indian dishes are very regional in character as they have been influenced by three factors. *firstly*, historical, which means that while the North was conquered and dominated by the Iranians, Afghans and Mughals for the last thousand years, it also means that their culture, language and food was adapted to the Indian way of life. This brought in the meat, chicken, pheasant, partridge and other non-vegetarian food in its **'Tandoori'** and rich **'Mughlai'** style of cooking with cream, yoghurt, almonds, and raisins, along with the Muslim **'Biryaanis'** which is basically exotic rice dishes with spices and meat. The Muslims were never able to dominate the south, so the south retained its vegetarianism right up till the nineteenth century when the Europeans came via the sea. The ports through which they made their entry became cosmopolitan cities like, Mumbai, Chennai and Kolkutta which embraced cuisines from all over the country; even Europe; vegetarian and non vegetarian. The Portuguese retained their port Goa for three centuries, up till 1965; therefore the influence of the Portuguese cuisine is very strong in that province. But food from the heart of south India is still unfamiliar in the west and terms like *'Dosa'*, *'Idli'*, *'Sambhar'* or *'Upma'* go unrecognized, but the Europeans did introduce pork which has made their dishes 'particularly the ' *Pork Vindaloo'* famous.

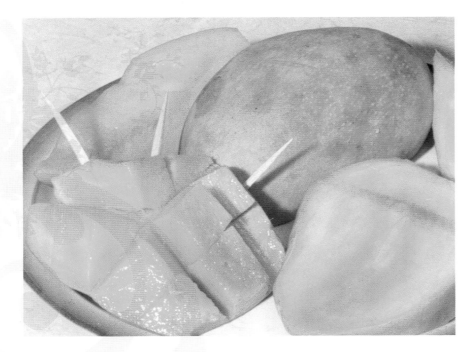

Secondly, geographically, there is a very large coastline from Bengal in the east, right round the southern tip and comes up to Mumbai in the west, which gives them a massive fish industry and a fish eating population. Needless to say the best fish dishes come from the south. The wet marshy ground is also good for growing the square rice which makes the south a rice eating region. The Panjab on the other hand is a wheat growing province which makes the north famous for its *'Naans'* and *'Rotis'* while the rice that grows in the foothills of the Himalayas is *'Basmati'*, the long grain variety, which, because of its ability to absorb the water while cooking, is ideal for the Mughal Biryaani dishes.

This leads me to the *third point; agriculture* also tends to influence regional cooking to a large extent; the corn and mustard crops in the Panjab gives it the most typical Panjabi meal of **'makki ki roti and sarson ka saag';** Bengal being situated in the Bay of Bengal and having marshy agricultural lands is well known for its *fish and rice;* the spices grown in the southern regions lead **the south Indian cooking tends to be very spicy;** the coconut growing province of Kerala *will have coconut base for all their curries;* and so the list goes on.

The Indian mango needs a special mention here as it is the one fruit which is available in the whole country; it can be used for a sweet or savoury in salads or shakes; it is used as a fruit; it is used in its raw form to make Chutneys and jams. It comes in dozens of varieties, the famous ones of which are; *'Dussehri'. 'Langda', 'Chausa'* or the most famous, *'Alphonso*. In Bengal you have the very small ones which can be eaten six at a time; in the south you have the very large ones which are fibrous, cannot be cut, need to be eaten whole, which can be a very messy job. **It comes in its raw form for only a fortnight in July when all the mango pickles and chutneys are made which last for the rest of the year.** Now, the mango here in the west is available, grown in the rest of the world; but the taste of the Indian mango still remains unique and the best.

Indian food is a careful synthesis and blend of spices, seasoning and flavours.

Its regional variations give this food a unique character. It also gives it a wide dimension to make it enjoyable to every taste. The secret of this art is to understand the various basic spices that go into this food and mix them accordingly to taste. This is a better formula than to use a pre-mixed dry curry powder or paste, as that way you cannot regulate the various flavours according to choice. Too much would make the curry hot, too little would give no flavours at all.

The properties and raw data of the spices and herbs can be got from any encyclopaedia or dictionary. **To know which brings out the best flavours of which meat or poultry or vegetable; at which stage it should be added to the curry** for the best result; or how much of which; therein lies the **art and the secret of Indian cooking.**

Some general points to note about Indian cookery and particularly about my recipes. **Firstly,** *the proportion of spices in my recipes is a general guide.* They can be adjusted to suit various tastes and increased or decreased as such; or if a particular spice is either not available or not liked, it can be omitted with little difference. **Secondly;** *the measure of water again is a rough guide* and can be increased or decreased depending upon whether you like a thin sauce; thick sauce; or a coating sauce. I also tend to use measures as opposed to weights as my friends found it easier to work with that than

An advisory note at the end; if you are a complete novice at Indian food and want to learn in a basic way, **start with the first six spices listed below, in their whole and ground forms; plus the tandoori masaala, rice and gram flour.** Learn the ingredients of the *'masaala'* paste of the fresh spicy and root herbs onion garlic, ginger, green chilli and coriander as a combination of this forms the basis of all Indian dishes. Cook with these and you will get good results; but be careful of the fact that the pungency of these fresh spices like the ginger, garlic or chilli or the size of the garlic cloves or the green or red chillies might be different. But practice in making the following recipes will allow you to make allowances for this factor. Then you can experiment with more ingredients.

All the following spices will be available in the Indian stores. Some local supermarkets or health food shops do carry some of the spices and some of the lentils and pulses, not all of them. The spices, whole or ground, individually or collectively are called 'masaalas'. This term is often repeated in the following recipes. **A point to note here; the term *'masaala'* is used for two formats; for the dry spice; or the mixture or paste of the fresh ingredient of onion/garlic/ginger/chillies, whether in the raw dorm or fried. This is a word of different formats that we grow up learning and understanding without being conscious of the learning process.**

Where the dry spices are concerned these can be kept in a round steel containers available in a 6", 8", or 10" diameter from the Indian stores. These spice containers are called 'Masaale ka dabba' which contain 7 small dishes inside the big container to hold the six basic spices and salt. This is a useful item to have and practical to use.

always having to bring the scales out. **Thirdly;** *there is no thickener used in Indian cooking,* be it flour or corn flower. *The thickness* of the sauce comes from the spices and the onion-tomato masaala. **Fourthly,** *there is generally no fresh sweet fruit, like apple or pineapple, used in traditional Indian curries;* the only exception being sultanas, cashew nuts, almonds and prunes, which are used in the Mughlai form of cooking to a large extent or the coconut which is the basis of south Indian food. **Very occasionally apple is used in Kashmiri food or pineapple in a few south Indian dishes. Fifthly,** the staple food in this cooking being rice or Indian bread, *potatoes is regarded as a vegetable and as such will be made into a curry,* dry spiced or roasted, just the same as any other vegetable.

Spices, Fresh Herbs, Lentils & other Ingredients

The six basic spices that I would recommend a novice to have on the shelves -

CORIANDER SEEDS: (SOOKHA DHANIA) — A product of India, these are seeds of the coriander plant and are used a lot in their ground form. You can buy them whole or ground, but to get the best flavour I would recommend you buy the whole seeds and grind them yourself in a sturdy electric coffee grinder. Store in an air tight jar.

CUMIN SEEDS: (JEERA) — An old well known spice, this is the seed of an annual plant, has a pleasant aroma but a slight bitter taste. Very popular in Indian food in whole and ground form. These can be bought both ways as the whole seeds are also used in quite a few dishes. For the ground, again I would recommend the do-it-yourself technique in the coffee grinder. If you can dry roast the cumin seeds and then grind them the flavours are far more distinct and certainly

more aromatic when sprinkled on top of dishes just before serving, particularly on the yoghurt dishes. The ordinary ground version is available in the local supermarkets but the whole seeds would generally be found only in the Indian stores.

FENUGREEK SEEDS: (METHRE) — Considered to be rich in carbohydrates and proteins these are from a Mediterranean plant, which now grows abundantly in India Also, has white flowers and pungent seeds. Yellow in colour, these are also used in forms, whole and ground. Keep both varieties on your shelf. For ground, same as above, grind in the coffee grinder and keep in an air-tight jar. A comparatively difficult spice to find; would be available in Indian stores only. An interesting fact to note here is that the fresh leaves of this plant called 'methi' are much used in Indian food; as a vegetable, cooked with potatoes or chicken; or added to curries as crushed leaves just for added flavour.

GARAM MASAALA: - There is no English name for this spice. It is a ground mix of a number of Indian spices and is available generally in Indian stores. It has very good digestive ingredients and sprinkling a pinch on most Indian dishes enhances the flavour as well. The ready mix of the store variety is not as potent as the home-made, as its pure form can be expensive. For the adventurous here are the proportions of the mix:-

      50 gms of black pepper
      10 gms. of seeds of black cardamoms
      10 gms. of cloves
      10 gms. of cinnamon sticks

Grind the above in the coffee grinder and store in an air-tight jar.

TURMERIC: (HALDI) - This is the yellow powder that gives curry its colour. It comes in a pre-packed form in the supermarket and Indian stores. In its original fresh form it can be thinly slices and used in salads; in its dry form it looks like dry ginger and is difficult to grind. It was known to have antiseptic properties; adding a pinch of turmeric to hot oil or ghee, making a paste and smearing it over wounds, cuts and boils to heal them faster. It is also good for digestion. Use it carefully as it can easily stain.

RED CHILLIES: (LAAL MIRCH) - This is the only one of the six that is actually hot so use it in proportion to the "heat" required in the dish. It can also be totally omitted or substituted for paprika to give the desired effect. It is useful to have the small dry red chillies in the larder cupboard, to give the garnishing on top of some lentil dishes, but mainly buy the ground variety in its pre-packed form. Since red chillies come in all different sizes and different strengths be careful and experiment with each new packet. Do not attempt to grind chillies yourself at home as they can make even the air pungent and sting the eyes. If you touch chillies with your fingers wash them well.

Four other pre-packed spices from Indian stores which would come in use are;

TANDOORI MASAALA - Basically a combination of the above spices and food colouring, for tandoori dishes. Not an original spice but a very convenient mixture to have on the shelves.

CHAAT MASAALA - A combination of some spices so constituted to give a tangy flavour to certain dishes of chaat and sometimes used to garnish the dry tandoori food. Again not an original spice; available in most Indian stores.

PAPRIKA - A very mild spice; ground red powder of certain red peppers. Not Indian in origin but I have found it to be very useful as a substitute for red chillies as it gives the colour without making the dish pungent.

AMCHUR - Dried raw mango powder - to give a tangy flavour, mostly to chutneys and 'Chaat', sometimes to chickpeas and potato curry.

Other Indian spices and dry fruits and nuts used are;

CARDAMOMS: (ILAICHI) — These are considered to be the third most expensive spice after saffron and vanilla. The seed pods of a tropical Asian plant, they come in two varieties. The big black pods are used in savoury dishes like rice, Biryaanis, meat and chicken. They are used whole and fried in oil at the start and at the end are served in the dish (not meant to be eaten). Cardamom seeds are used to make Garam Masaala. The small green pods are used more for sweet dishes - although they can be used in place of the black ones in case of necessity, but not vice versa. Both varieties also have immense medicinal properties, especially good for stomach cramps. Only available in Indian stores.

CLOVES: (LAUNG) — A widely traded spice, the dried flower bud of a tropical tree, the clove is very good as a mouth freshener and well known for its anaesthetic properties as biting on a clove on a painful tooth can be soothing. Whole cloves are used in rice and meat dishes, have a lovely aroma and are very helpful for indigestion. Widely available.

CINNAMON: (DAALCHEENI) - These are the shavings of the edible and aromatic inner and thin bark of a tree, generally grown in Southern India. They are best bought as sticks. Again they are used in meat and rice dishes, mainly for their aroma and herbal properties and can be eaten raw. Good for digestion; commonly found in all local shops.

WHOLE RED CHILLIES: (SAABAT LAAL MIRCH) - These are small and pungent, but full of flavour when dropped in sizzling hot oil. Use for garnishing, but use sparingly and remember to wash your hands well if you touch them. Available only in Indian shops.

BLACK CUMMIN SEEDS: (SHAH JEERA) - A variation of the above cumin seed, but greyish black in colour and more pungent in flavour. Generally used in its whole form for rice dishes, biryaanis and chutneys Also called 'kaala Jeera' which basically means black cumin, it is available in specialized stores only.

ONION SEEDS: (KALONJI) - These are black in colour and mainly used for chutneys, fish dishes or sprinkling on top of naans. They are called onion seeds here but do not confuse them with the onion growing variety from the local flower nurseries as they are not the eating ones. These are available only in the Indian stores.

MUSTARD SEEDS: (SARSON) - Small, round black seeds, they are nutty in flavour and sizzle when dropped in oil. They have a lovely, unusual aroma, used mainly in South Indian food and make a good combination with the curry leaves.
They come in three varieties; white, brown and black mustard. It is the black that is used in Indian food and is generally found in the specialized stores only.

RAI - There is no English name for these small round black seeds, similar in appearance to the mustard seeds but much smaller in size. Once crushed they have tangy properties, and are used in making most pickles, sometimes chutneys also. Available from the Indian stores only.

SESAME SEEDS: (TIL) - An Asian plant that yields oil bearing seeds which in their seed form can be used for flavouring in Indian breads, naans or mathis. Available in most local health food shops..

POMEGRANATE SEEDS: (ANAARDANA) - These are the dried seeds of the pomegranate fruit. It has a tangy flavour, used in chutneys, 'Raitas', salads or the chickpea dishes. Generally available only in the Indian stores.

POPPY SEEDS: (KHASKHAS) - Different to the seeds here as these are lighter in colour. Used for pickles and chutneys and sometimes for topping Naans and Rotis. Again, the seeds have herbal properties but available in specialized stores only.

BISHOP'S WEED: (AJVAIN) — Mainly cultivated in India these are light brown in colour, look very much like cumin seeds, but have a totally different flavour. They are generally kneaded in the dough of snacks like 'Samosas', or 'Mathis', sometimes in the dough of 'Pooris', occasionally used in curries and marinades, or even made into a cold drink. They have immense medicinal properties, good for wind or cramps in the stomach; can be found in specialized stores only.

TAMARIND: (IMLI) - Tamarind is a tropical evergreen tree bearing a pulpy fruit but with a firm exterior. The fruit is brown in colour and is sold in a dry pre-packed form in the Indian stores only. Mainly used for chutneys, occasionally for a lentil curry, it is tangy in taste and has to be soaked and sieved as a thick paste to get the best results.

CURRY LEAVES: (KARI PATTA) - These are the leaves of a plant, similar to a bay leaf and can be dried and stored in an air-tight jar. Well known for its flavour, particularly for lentils and South Indian dishes. The aroma of fresh leaves is excellent and most houses in India will have a tree growing in the back yard for utility and for its fragrance. The fresh and dried varieties can be found in Indian stores.

BAY LEAF: (TEJ PATTA) - The leaf of a laurel plant, dried and used as a flavouring in rice, meat and Biryaani dishes. The Indian variety is far more pungent than the western and will give a strong flavour in a curry, so use with care. Easily available as it is used in western food as well.

NUTMEG; (JAIPHAL) — An old Indian spice, mentioned in the Vedic literature it has great importance in the Ayurvedic medicine. Commercially produced in India, it is the fruit of an evergreen tree. An expensive spice, but it has great properties for digestion. Use sparingly in meat or chicken dishes. The spice is the kernel which is a difficult nut to grind so always take the powdered variety. Generally available.

MACE; (JAVATRI) — Nutmeg and mace are unique spices as they come from the same tree. Mace is reddish brown, sometimes flame orange, in colour, the dried bark like covering that is round the inner kernel of nutmeg Since mace is paper thin and brittle they require different treatments and end up as different spices and aromas even though the properties are similar. Again the flavouring of this spice is effective in non-vegetarian dishes. In its whole form it is available in specialized stores only.

ASAFOETIDA: (HEENG) - This is the gum of a Persian plant. It has tremendous herbal and medicinal properties. It has a very strong piercing aroma and flavour, so a very minute quantity is required for a dish, usually a pinch is sufficient. Being extremely strong the flavour is not always liked. So experiment with caution. Remember to wash your fingers well after using it or the smell could linger for a long time. Available in Indian stores only.

DRIED MUSHROOMS: (GUCHIAN, OR DHINGRI) - These are dried mushrooms, difficult to find and expensive to buy, as this variety is found only in either Kashmir or Afghanistan. If you do find them they are delicious. Wash well and soak before use to bring up the volume. Used in vegetarian curries and rice dishes. Found in specialized stores only.

RAISINS; (KISHMISH): Slim, long, seedless grapes, dried naturally which give it these grapes a different flavour and texture to the spun dried ones which are used in the west. Originally the good variety came only from the Middle East. Kishmish has a distinct taste of its own and suits Indian dishes better than the raisins. Generally used in sweet dishes but in Kashmir and Rajasthan it is also used for their rice and meat dishes as well. Available, with difficulty, in large Indian stores only.

PISTACHIO: (PISTA) - Nut of a tree found in Mediterranean countries and western Asia. An expensive, but popular dry fruit in India. It has a hard white shell on the outside with a small green nut on the inside. Used mainly in sweet dishes.

CASHEW NUTS: (KAAJU) - Off white in colour, these are Kidney shaped nuts. By and large, a product of Southern India, these nuts grow on trees. Each one is encased in a very hard shell, which makes the shelling and processing of these expensive. Very popular in Indian food, savoury and sweet, particularly for the Indian style pastry called 'Burfi', even served as snacks on their own, just as they are, or lightly fried and salted.

ALMONDS; (BADAAM) — Reddish brown in colour, these nuts are popular in the east and west. Highly nutritious. In the winter they are used whole with their brown skin. In the summer they can be soaked, peeled and then ground into a paste and made into a refreshing summers drink called 'Sardyayi' which is very cooling for the body.

CHILGOZA; Brown in colour these nuts have no English name. They are like pine nuts in shape and size and sometimes confused with them but they have a stronger taste than pine nuts, are good for health in the winter, and used mainly in sweets. Available only in very specialized stores.

VERMICELLI: (SEVIAN) - This is the Indian version which is finer than the Pakistani or the American version. My grandmother would make these vermicelli strands by hand, out of flour dough, dry them in the sun, store them and then make the nicest sweet with them. The idea is still the same except they are now commercially made. It is available in large supermarkets but to get the authentic Indian product you might have to visit the Indian shop.

JAGGERY: (GUR) - Unrefined cane sugar it has a distinct taste of its own It is sold in small lumps of various sizes, sometimes plain, and sometimes with ginger, nuts ajvain or fennel seed added in. Can be eaten plain, in yoghurt as a sweet, used in pickles and chutneys or cooked in rice. Very versatile ingredient, available only in Indian shops.

SAFFRON: (KESAR) - . Called the 'golden spice' it has a mild rust colour and an exquisite aroma These are the dried petals of a flower originally found in Kashmir, is very expensive, difficult to obtain, and used sparingly. It is now more readily available since these flowers are now grown in Spain on a commercial basis. It is used in sweet and savoury dishes both for its flavour and colour. To get the best out of the petals, soak them in a few spoons of warm milk or water for 2-3 hours and then use the liquid. Widely available.

SILVER LEAF: (VARK) - Used purely for decoration purposes, this leaf, as the name denotes, is actually made with pure silver. Tissue paper thin, it is nevertheless edible. Very delicate, it is packed in between sheets of greaseproof paper, and should be lifted with the support paper to put on the top of a dish. Then, remember to discard the paper. An expensive ingredient it should be stored in an airtight container. A variation of this is the gold leaf which being expensive is seldom used. Available only in large specialized stores.

AFTER DINNER FRESHENERS;

At the end of an Indian meal you could serve any one or more of the following two after dinner fresheners instead of mints;

FENNEL SEEDS: (SONF) - A European herb of the carrot family, grown for its foliage and aromatic seeds. The seeds are small, green and oval and come in two sizes, normal and small. The first is called just 'Sonf' or Fennel seed and is sometimes brewed in Indian tea, occasionally used in marinades, curries, even a sweet. The second, called 'Lucknavi Sonf,' or 'Aniseed' is the one generally served in restaurants at the end of a meal, with small bits of crystal sugar to enhance the taste. Again a very valuable herb as it has great medicinal properties and helps digestion. It eases stomach cramps, cures wheezing and may stop hiccups. Available in specialized stores only.

SUPAARI: These are the shavings of the betel nut, which is an areca nut. They are either packaged just on their own or sometimes mixed with minute sugar crystals or finely chopped dry fruit. There are a number of varieties of supaari some of which may be available in Indian stores only.

CHOORAN; A tangy taste, made with herbs and spices, this has digestive properties and therefore very popular. It has a number of variations in its composition, taste and manner of serving. It can be packaged in different sizes of sucking sweets; spicy and tangy, mild or strong. Available in specialized stores only.

COOKING OILS;

You can use any of the commercial cooking oils for Indian food. However, the two cooking mediums, of which you might have heard of, and which are Indian by application are;

GHEE: This is just clarified butter. It is made by simply simmering the butter on a low heat, burning up the residue of the butter, and then bottling the clear oil while it is still warm. This has two advantages; firstly the clear butter can be stored for at least a year; secondly, there will not be burnt residue at the bottom of a pan every time you start to make a dish. Indian curries made in this ghee have a superb flavour. Tinned ghee is also available.

MUSTARD OIL: (SARSON KA TEL) - Very pungent and inedible in its raw form; but once heated to a high temperature, till there is a slight haze in the oil, and then cooled and used, it has a lovely flavour. It is mainly used for frying and the best 'Pakoras' are made in it. In Bengal it is used for fish, in the Panjab for 'Pooris' and in its raw form it is used, throughout India, for pickles and chutneys.

PULSES AND LENTILS; (DAALS)

Known by either name, these are the edible seeds of several leguminous plants and are the basic groundwork of Indian cookery. Inexpensive to buy, these are high in proteins and nutritional value and an excellent substitute for meat.

There are five main groups of Lentils;

URAD KI DAAL; Black in colour whether cooked or uncooked. It comes in three forms; whole, split and washed. Of these, the most famous is the whole variety which is also known as Kale maan; Very famous in the Panjab and Delhi region and is often part of the exotic Indian culinary scene.

MOONG KI DAAL; Green in colour cooked and uncooked, it comes in three forms; whole, split and washed. The washed variety is yellow in colour. All the three forms have their own different taste when cooked.

MASAR KI DAAL; Comes in three forms, the whole, the split and the washed; pinkish red in colour when in the packet, yellow when cooked. The washed is best known as it is commonly used for soups in the west and available in nearly every local supermarket.

ARHAR KI DAAL; Yellow in colour whether cooked Or uncooked. Mostly used in South India, it is the only lentil popularly cooked with vegetables in it.

CHANNE KI DAAL; Again yellow in colour cooked and uncooked. It is a favourite of the Panjab region, and used to be termed as the poor mans daal.
As children we found the names of the various daals very confusing and always referred to them by their colours which were always fascinating. These lentils are all available in the health food shops.

Other seeds in this group, although slightly different to the above are the beans and peas variety and are mainly three in number;

KIDNEY BEANS; (RAJMAAN) - Red kidney shaped beans, these used to be grown mainly in the Kashmir region in the very north of India. Very traditional in Indian food, they have now been discovered by the west and have become part of the healthy eating scene, as they are very high in nutritional value. Now they are widely available.

CHICKPEAS; (CHANNAS) - Beige in colour these are round in shape and very hard in texture. They are very popular in the north of India and like the Kidney beans have become part of the healthy food spectrum here in the west. They are widely available.

BLACK EYED BEANS; (RONGI) - Cream coloured kidney shaped beans with a black dot in the middle of it hence the name. Again, since these are high in protein value they are being stocked by the health food shops, although they have never been as popular as the above two, either here or in Indian food. .

INDIAN RICE AND FLOUR;

Indian curries are always accompanied by rice or an Indian bread which can be either Chapaathi, Naan or Poori, which are all made with either plain flour, the wide availability of which here in the west makes a discussion of it irrelevant here, or chapaathi flour;

RICE; (CHAAVAL) - The most popular variety of North Indian rice is Basmati rice. It is different in texture to the American or English rice or even Patna rice which is high in starch. Basmati rice is slim, long grained with little starch and is the only rice which, with the correct proportion of water can be cooked without having to drain it as the water is absorbed leaving the grains fluffy and separate. Ideal for making pulao and Biryaani.

CHAPAATHI FLOUR; (ATTA) - Marketed under this name, and available in Indian stores this flour is a mixture of wheaten and plain. It is high in fibre, used for Indian breads called Chapaathis, Rotis, Pooris or Paranthas. Naans are made with plain flour. Eaten with curry as a substitute for rice and is as popular in the North of India as rice is in the south.

CORN FLOUR; (MAKKI KA ATTA) - A produce of the Panjab, this flour is different in taste and texture to the corn flour available here. This flour makes a very interesting variety of bread and is occasionally used in the cooking of vegetables. Available in the larger Indian stores only.

GRAM FLOUR; (BESAN) - It is the ground form of a lentil called Channe ki daal and is slightly yellow in colour. Rich in protein it is used for batter in Indian cooking. Famous for making pakoras and bhajis, two of the more well known of Indian savouries, sometimes as a thickener, occasionally in a curry. Available in most Indian stores.

SEMOLINA; (SOOJI) - These are the coarse particles left after the sifting of wheat. Sooji is a form of semolina, white in colour, finer than the one here. The ordinary Semolina can be substituted for Sooji, but I have always noticed that the dishes made with Sooji have a more distinct flavour. It is not easily available and you might have to try the large Indian stores for it.

FRESH INGREDIENTS;

So far we talked of the dry ingredients, including the ground spices, which I called Masaalas. Now we will discuss the basic step of a curry which is also called Masaala, but this is a Masaala paste which is generally a proportion of onion, ginger and garlic with a touch of green chillies, sometimes fresh coriander. All these are either put into a food processor and processed, or chopped very finely. They are then fried until golden brown in colour and set aside. Some of these little known fresh Indian ingredients are;

GINGER; (ADARAK) - The root of a tropical plant, it is now widely available. Very good for digestion, it is very widely used in Indian cooking even in drinks. It should be peeled before use. It can be stored in a cool place for weeks or alternatively it can be peeled and frozen in inch cube pieces.

GARLIC; (LASAN) - Again the root of a plant which is sold as small bulbs. The cloves have to be separated and peeled before crushing or slicing them. The size of the garlic cloves differs enormously depending on the county of its origin. The garlic in India has small cloves; the ones here are sometimes four times its size. I have taken the cloves to be of medium size in my recipes; you can increase or decrease according to the bulb you are working with. It has herbal properties, good for digestion, but use with care as it has a strong flavour, in fact some people do not use this spice because of the strong flavour. Always wash your hands well after using garlic or the smell will stay for a long time.

GREEN CHILLIES; (HARI MIRCH) - These have a lovely flavour, but use sparingly as they can be very hot. They come in all shapes and sizes and are used in different cuisines; Thai, Mexican, Chinese and Indian. The small green chillies are the Indian or Thai variety, are particularly pungent, and are sold in most supermarkets...

CORIANDER; (DHANIA) - A leafy herb, much like parsley, was used in ancient medicinal preparations, now used for flavouring and garnishing. Can be substituted by parsley if required, but I have found that if I have used parsley on an Indian dish it does the trick for the looks, but it does little to enhance the flavour. But then if I have used coriander on an English stew or casserole in place of parsley it has not done justice to that either. .

MINT; (PUDEENA) - An aromatic herb. Used mainly for chutneys and marinades. Fresh or dried leaves can be used although the former are more fragrant. Widely available.

COCONUT; (NARIYAL) - A large hard shelled nut with a white inner kernel which has water in it of a refreshing mild taste. It makes a good summer drink. The kernel is grated and used in most south Indian dishes. Also comes in a pre-packed dry packet called creamed coconut, which when dissolved in hot boiling water makes coconut milk. Both are available in supermarkets, former fresh coconut with fresh vegetables and latter as creamed coconut on the shelves with chutneys and pickles.

ACCOMPANIMENTS;

POPPADUMS: (PAAPARS) - These are thin, dry pancake shaped rounds, sold in pre-packed forms in Indian stores and now in some large supermarkets also. Made with dough of dried ground lentils, seasoned with red chillies, ground black pepper or garlic, these rounds are then dried naturally, in the hot sun, a technique that makes it very difficult to make these here at home. The commercial varieties are good, follow the directions on the packets, as they can be either grilled or deep-fried. An excellent nibble, to serve with drinks before an Indian meal or even with the meal itself. Not to be confused with Indian breads, as I have seen Poppadums being served wrongly in lieu of the bread.

PICKLES AND CHUTNEYS: (ACHAARS) - An interesting part of an Indian meal. Recipes for some pickles and chutneys have been included in this book; but for those who are novices, there are now a variety of good commercial pickles in the market. You can chose from pickled mango, lime, brinjal, garlic, mixed or even mango chutney, all of which are nice. Choose one to your taste. They also come labelled as mild, medium or hot, relating to the chilli part of it, so choose with care. Remember to have a very slight bit with each mouthful to get just the flavour of the pickle each time; no more.

Serving Food Indian Style

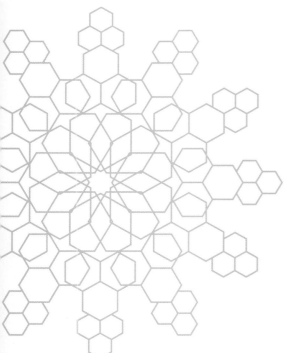

The technique of serving Indian food is somewhat different to that of serving western food. **Traditionally there are no starters. If entertaining there could be finger snacks passed round with chutneys during drinks; in the winter there could be hot soup served in a cup. Restaurants, who have adopted the modern concept of appetisers as a course would use the recipes from the snacks and savouries section or the tandoori, and serve them in small portion.**

For a main family meal, there is one curried dish, be it a meat, vegetable or Daal, with a side dry spicy dish, which is complementary to the main one; e.g. if the curry is a meat dish then the side can be a dry roasted vegetable; if the main is a Daal, then the side can be dry roasted meat or a vegetable; if the main is a vegetable then you can have even a dry Daal. The accompaniments would be a plain yoghurt or a *'Raita'*, rice or a simple Indian bread like a *'Chapaathi'*, maybe even both, and a

pickle or chutney. For an evening party you can make as many dishes as you like or rather are able to; but generally you would do at least a meat or chicken dish, a daal, a vegetable and maybe, either a fish or a paneer dish. The accompaniments would be the same, yoghurt, rice, some form of Indian bread, variety of pickles and chutneys and then add a salad, preferably green or a plain onion and tomato, and Poppadums. These are laid out in the centre of the table in dishes from which everybody just serves themselves.

To give individual servings put some rice on the side of a dinner plate, add the main dish, if it is meat or chicken with a thick sauce, on the side of it and then add the dry dish beside it. **Do not ladle any thing on top of the rice** as we prefer to eat each spoonful of the rice with a different flavour. Daal and yoghurt is traditionally served in small steel or glass bowls and set beside the plate on the right side, while serving the bread on the side plate onto the left. A spoonful of the pickle can be set on a corner of the main plate or even on the side plate from which take a small bit with each spoonful of rice or piece of bread.

In south India traditionally a 'thali' is served. Thali literally means a large steel plate; in terms of serving food it means 6-7 small dishes called .'katories' are filled with various dishes; curries, yoghurts, rice, salad sometimes even a

sweet, and arranged on this plate with chapaathis in the middle and a small glass of water on the side. This is a very convenient way of serving Indian food.

Traditionally there **may** be one sweet, but not always so. Sometimes the meal may be finished by putting jaggery or sugar on a chapaathi with a dollop of cream or its Indian equivalent, malai on it, rolling it up and eating it; or having a piece of burfi. For a party there is generally one; going to two at the very most; three would be an overstatement.

As you would realize, it is very difficult to be accurate in quantity, in our meals. We tend to cook more than required, as I particularly would always remember my father's words that 'food must never be finished

on the table, as someone might still be hungry, or worse, an unexpected visitor might have to go hungry.' An Irish friend of my twin sons, through his school years, often came to us for his evening meal. As we tend to eat late in the evening, about eight o'clock, which is reminiscent of our life in India where the mealtime is even later, this friend use to joke and say that if he worked his strategy well he could have his evening tea in his own home at about 6 o'clock and then arrive with us a couple of hours later for a second meal as there was always extra for a visitor on our table. But, if you are left with extras, put them in small covered dishes and keep in the fridge. They can be heated the next day in the microwave extremely well. Rice fluffs up beautifully, but be careful with Indian breads as they tend to dry up. They are better heated under the grill.

Namkeen
(Snacks, Savouries & Starters)

Pakoras
(Deep fried vegetables coated in Gram flour batter)
Samosas
(Deep fried patties filled with Potatoes and Peas)
Vadas
(Savouries made with Lentil batter)
Aalu ki Tikki
(Small round spicy Potato cakes)
Shammi Kebabs
(Minced Lamb Kebabs)

Section

The Indians, as a whole, are very fond of snacks and savouries. They can be seen in buses and streets munching them, very much in the same manner that the western world munches chocolates and biscuits whenever and wherever. If you walk down a busy street in Delhi, you will see open stalls on both sides of the road, sometimes even on large trolleys, frying hot 'Samosas' or 'Pakoras', and you will be tempted to buy them there and then, coming off the hot stove. You will get them in disposable plates, or even on a plate made of banana leaves, again disposable, but very traditional, and eat the delicious snacks while walking down the road. In the summer months you would see Fruit chaat' or 'Paapri chaat', or 'Gol-guppas', all of which are chilli-hot and tangy, ideal for the hot climate; in the winter you could see griddles with 'Aalu ki Tikkis' on them, very much like potato burgers, which are cooked in front of you and then handed over in a disposable saucer as it would hold chutney and maybe spicy chickpeas as well. In winter the street vendors will sell all sorts of 'Tikkas', 'Kebabs', fish, meat or chicken. In the corn season, you could see small, cheap make-shift barbecues on the pavements, where you can choose your own corn on the cob. It will be roasted while you wait and then will have salt, ground black pepper and fresh lemon juice sprinkled on it. You can go away with the bag of hot cob tucked under your arm or, or on a piece of old newspaper, so that you can eat it on your way to the shops. In Bombay there will be 'Bhelpuri' or 'Aalu chaat', even raw coconut, the water of which is drunk through a straw before the soft cream like flesh is scooped out and given to you in a dish.

Samosas and Pakoras, which sometimes are called 'bhajis' are the two that have been popularized by the supermarkets here in the west as they have appeared in their ready made snacks line. Both are easy to make with their ingredients fairly available; for Pakoras you would need gram flour as opposed to ordinary flour but it should be available in any Indian grocery store. After that, with imagination at hand, the sizes and fillings of either could be varied to suit any taste and for any meal.

The ideal cooking utensils for most Indian snacks would be a 'Karaahi' - a Balti-cum-Wok type of a pan, ideal for deep frying, and is also discussed in the section on breads. A heavy based griddle, aluminium or cast iron, would be appropriate for shallow frying. If either or both are unavailable then a heavy based saucepan with deep sides could be used.

Due to the climate in India the timings of meals would be different to those in the west. A siesta in the afternoons, after lunch, is a must when work generally comes to a standstill; in some areas even shops close for a couple of hours. Then, evening starts with a cup of tea at 4.30-5.30pm, when snacks are served; the full evening meal is put back to 8.30-9pm. In practical terms it can be said that the supper in the west is our evening tea, the actual meal being served at suppertime. Also, culturally speaking, cocktail parties are very popular in India, and even otherwise, the emphasis on before dinner nibbles, even if there is going to be a full laid out meal, makes this section quite important and interesting. The same nibbles are now served as starters in the west, but be careful of the quantities as they can be quite filling. Tandoori dishes of the next section are also good as appetisers as long as their quantity is reduced.

PAKORAS

(Deep fried vegetables coated in Gram flour batter);

Variation

To make Chicken Pakoras cut strips or squares of roasted chicken and put into gram flour batter. Fry in hot oil as chicken is already cooked.

To make egg pakoras, hard boil the eggs and cut slice into quarters; salt & pepper the pieces, coat with batter and fry in hot oil.

There is no English name for this extremely popular Indian snack/savoury. It is often labelled as 'bhajis' in the supermarkets but this is a colloquial term. It *is a favourite of the whole country*, although each region will use different spices in the batter or make slight variations. It can suit everyone's taste as pakoras can be made with most **vegetables**, sliced or chopped; they can be **non-vegetarian**, the chicken pakoras and the fish pakoras being the top of this range; they can be exotic with diced Paneer or soft Paneer with spices, shaped into small round balls. Pakoras can be had at breakfast, as an accompaniment to eggs; they can be had for evening tea; served at cocktail parties; or added to the menu of a set buffet. Opposite is a basic recipe; I have taken a small selection to give a flavour of this dish.

Recipe; Makes about 25-30 pakoras, depending on the size of the vegetables

Ingredients

2 medium sized potatoes, washed and peeled

1 small onion, peeled

1 small aubergine, washed

3 medium sized tomatoes, washed

8 small cubes of paneer

1/2 spoon of salt

1/2 spoon of garam masaala

Oil for deep frying

Batter;

2 cups of gram flour, sieved

1/2 teaspoon of baking powder

1/2 teaspoon of salt

Pinch of paprika

Pinch of garam masaala

4 sprigs of fresh coriander, finely chopped

1 small green chilli, finely chopped

1/2 -1 cup of water

For garnishing;

3 sprigs of fresh coriander or parsley, chopped and a pinch of amchur

Method

(1) **First make the batter.** Take the gram flour, baking powder and salt, and mix them well. Add the water bit by bit and keep mixing by hand till you reach a thickish consistency; something like a pancake batter consistency. Now sprinkle the pinch of paprika and the garam masaala, add the chopped coriander and the green chilli, mix well again, cover and set aside.

(2) **Prepare the vegetables.** Slice the potatoes to a thickness of about 1/6 inch thick. Slice the onions a bit thicker than the potatoes. Slice the aubergine, with the skin on, again to the thickness of about 1/4 inch. Halve the tomatoes.

(3) Heat the oil in a karaahi or a wok on a medium heat.

(4) While the oil is heating, rub the salt, garam masaala, paprika or red chillies onto both sides of the vegetables and the paneer.

(5) Check if the oil is hot enough by dropping a spoon of the batter in the oil. It should take a minute or so to brown. Now, you are ready to dip the vegetables in the batter; make sure they are coated on both sides and drop them in the hot oil. Start with the potatoes, as they will need to cook; so check that the heat is on medium to low as the potatoes will need 5-6 mins to cook. When golden brown on both sides, take them out and drain on kitchen paper. Finish making all the potato slices the same way. Then do the same for aubergines; as they will also need the same time to cook. When you come to the onions and the paneer, put the heat up as there is nothing in them that require cooking. Put in the tomatoes last and do the same for them as for the onion.

(6) Arrange them on a flat dish, garnish and serve hot.

Garnish;

with amchur and fresh coriander or parsley, chopped

Serve; with tomato chutney, mint chutney, or sonth; they can also be rolled in chapaatis; or they can be put into a bap with any of the above chutneys or even tomato ketchup and made into a pakora burger; serve as a snack or starter.

Overall cooking time; 1 to 1 1/2hours.

Mom's Tips

(1) If there is no karaahi or wok available, use a frying pan with deep sides so that the oil does not splash out when the vegetables are being dropped in.

(2) Do not skin the aubergines, or courgettes if using them, as then the crunch bite is absent from the finished pakora.

(3) **Do not salt the vegetables** till the oil is heating and you are ready to cook the pakoras or it will soften the vegetables.

(4) Always put in the vegetables which need to be cooked first as they will take time; if using tomatoes, put them in last, as they tend to give out a little water in the oil.

(5) You can take the pakoras out before they turn golden brown, making sure the vegetables are cooked; these can then be put back in hot oil for 1 min. to finish off cooking before serving them. *If you need to reheat at a later stage do so under the grill,* not in the microwave, or they will turn soggy.

(6) Not a good dish for freezing, as the pakoras tend to become soggy when defrosted.

SAMOSAS

(Deep fried patties filled with Potatoes and Peas);

Samosas are a well known Indian snack, popular in Britain, particularly since it is on the shelves of the large chain stores. *A dish of the north or south of India* with slight variations, the samosa is a snack available with the roadside vendors, office canteens, home parties, family treats. It can be bought on its own, wrapped up in a newspaper, it can be had with tomato chutney or a mint chutney; children love it with plain tomato sauce; or it can be made into a lunch time snack with channas on the side; it can be part of a party buffet; or it can be made into cocktail size and served with pre-dinner drinks. It can be *vegetarian or non-vegetarian;* it can be stuffed with Indian style dry vegetable; or with English style ham and cheese. **With imagination and flair it can be varied immensely.** Opposite is the traditional recipe of samosas, stuffed with spiced potatoes and peas.

Recipe; Makes 10-12 samosas

Ingredients

Dough;

2 cups of plain flour, sieved

1/4 cup of cold cooking oil

Pinch of salt

Pinch of ajvain (optional)

1/2 cup of water, approximately

Filling;

6 medium sized potatoes, boiled and peeled

1 cup of shelled or frozen peas

1 large onion, chopped

2-3 small green chillies, finely chopped

7-8 sprigs of fresh coriander, chopped

1 teaspoon of garam masaala

1/2 teaspoon of paprika

1/2 teaspoon of red chillies

1 teaspoon of salt

1 teaspoon of chaat masaala or amchur

1 tablespoon of lemon juice

3 tablespoons of cooking oil

Oil for deep frying

For garnishing;

6 small red tomatoes

Method

(1) **First make the filling.** Dice the boiled and peeled potatoes into very small pieces. Set them aside.

(2) Heat the three tablespoons of oil in a karaahi or a broad heavy based frying pan and fry the onions till they are golden brown. Add the green chillies and the coriander and mix well. Add peas and cook for 2-3 mins, add garam masaala, paprika, red chillies and salt and mix.

(3) Put in the diced potatoes, chaat masaala or amchur and the lemon juice and mix thoroughly. Taste the mixture for salt and chillies and then set aside to cool

(4) **Now make the dough.** Put in the plain flour, the oil, salt and ajvain into a food processor and make firm dough.

(5) Put the tava or a heavy based pan on a very low heat. Divide the dough into 10-12 portions. Grease a rolling board and roll each one out to a diameter of about 8-10 inches, and set them on the working top, side by side. Put each round on the warm tava for about 10 seconds, do not turn over, just take it off the tava, and stack them in a tea towel. Keep them well covered to keep warm.

(6) Make a light paste with one tablespoon of plain flour and two tablespoons of water in a small dish. Then put one round on the rolling board, cut it into half. Holding one half in your left hand, with the cooked side on the inside, make a cone of it, put a spoon of the cold filling and then seal the edges with the flour paste. Set it on a greased surface while the rest are made the same way. Keep them covered with a damp tea towel so that they do not dry out.

(7) Heat the oil for frying in a karaahi or wok on a medium heat. Drop in the prepared samosas 3-4 at a time, brown them slowly as the pastry has to cook. It should take 4-5 mins for each batch. Drain on kitchen paper; arrange on a flat dish and serve hot.

Garnish;

Tradionally there is no garnish on the samosas; but you can set the small red tomatoes on top of the samosas to add a little colour.

Serve; As a snack or starter with sonth, tomato chutney, mint chutney, any relish or even tomato sauce; or with channas on the side with any of the above chutneys.

Overall cooking time: 1 hour and 30 mins.

Mom's Tips

(1) The dough must be very firm or it will be difficult to work with.

(2) If making a large batch, take them out of the oil just before they become golden in colour. Then, just before serving put them back in for about 20 seconds each side and they will then be all hot.

(3) Once you learn to make the samosas you can try out **any filling** you like, as long as it is dry and is cut up into small pieces. You can also make the size of the *samosas as large or as small as you like.*

(4) A great dish for freezing. The samosas can be frozen after step (6); before frying them. Freeze them individually, then put them together in a box; take out as many as required at a time. Lightly defrost them, and then finish off frying them as in the last step before serving them. If reheating, do so in the grill, not in the microwave, as the pastry tends to become soft in it.

VADAS

(Savouries made with Lentil batter);

This dish is unique in the sense that it can be claimed as a dish by the North of India and by the South; the difference lies in its presentation; it is made as a yoghurt dish in the north, but it is had with a lentil curry in the south. But in my young days I remember being in the kitchen and enjoying them just as they were being fried, and through the years I have introduced these as such to my friends, sons and now grandchildren who have had them as a savoury with drinks, as a starter with the meal, as a snack at supper, even as an accompaniment to eggs at breakfast and liked them at all times.

Recipe; Makes 10-12 vadas, 20-25 small drops.

Ingredients

1 glass of washed Urad lentil

1 medium sized onion, peeled (optional)

1 inch cube of ginger, peeled

1-2 green chillies

5-6 sprigs of fresh coriander

1/4 teaspoon of red chillies

1/2 teaspoon of garam masaala

Pinch of asafoetida (heing)

1/4 teaspoon of baking powder

1/4 teaspoon of salt

3-4 tablespoons of water

Oil for deep frying

For garnishing;

2 red chillies, 1 green chilli

Method

(1) **First prepare the Batter.** Wash the lentil well and soak it in plenty of water for at least 6-8 hours. Then drain the water, wash the lentil again, and put into a food processor. Add 2-3 tablespoons of water and if required put in more water when making the batter, which should be a drop scone consistency. The lentil should be well processed so that if rubbed between two fingers it should feel just a bit gritty, like sugar. Take it out and put it into a mixing bowl

(2) **Now prepare the rest of the ingredients.** Cut the onion, ginger, chillies and coriander very finely; you can even gently process them in the food processor before making the batter.

(3) Mix them into the batter thoroughly. Then add the dry spices, red chillies, garam masaala, asafoetida and salt and mix gain. Put in the baking powder also and keep mixing for about 5 minutes. This makes the batter light and that will make softer vadas.

(4) Heat the oil in a karaahi or a wok on a medium heat. Then make the vadas. There are two different ways to make them. First the traditional way; wet the palm of your hands, put a tablespoon of the batter in the centre of your left hand, and with the right hand flatten it out to a diameter of about 3 inches. Then make a hole in the centre and gently ease off the vada from your palm into the hot oil. Make 3-4 more and keep sliding them into the oil. By now the first would need to be turned over. The oil should not be too hot as these should take about 6-8 mins to be cooked through. The second and easier way to make these is just to drop a spoonful of batter into the hot oil and make 10-12 per batch. These should only take 4-5 mins to cook. Keep the first batch warm while making the second. Arrange them on a flat dish, garnish and serve hot.

Garnish;

Traditionally there is no garnish but you can arrange the red and green chillies in the centre of the dish.

Serve;

As a snack or starter with Mint or coconut chutney for a snack for afternoon tea or suppertime; or at breakfast, as an accompaniment to fried eggs, particularly for vegetarians.

Overall cooking time:

1 to 1hour and 15min.

Mom's Tips

(1) The lentil must be soaked for the required length of time as it has to be soft enough to be ground well. The mixing of the batter by hand is also very important or the vadas will not turn out to be as soft as they should.

(2) Remember to keep the heat at medium even reducing it to low if required, as the vadas are cooking, because they are easy to brown but at the same time the lentil has to be cooked through.

(3) A very good dish to freeze. Make a large batch and freeze, and take out as many as required at a time. They can be reheated under the grill or drop them in hot oil for 30 secs.

AALU KI TIKKI

(Small round spicy Potato cakes);

Variation

Fry have a cup of peas in 1 tablespoon of oil for 3-4 mins and cool them, add a pinch of salt, pinch of red chillies and a chopped green chilli. Put 3-4 peas in the centre of shaped potato Tikki in step (4) then fry them.

A popular snack enjoyed in the whole country; *but more so in the Panjab, Delhi and Uttar Pradesh, which comprise the north of India.* It can be had on its own as a snack; with a cup of tea; with cocktails; as part of a main spread of a meal. It can be added to the chaat group of foods and had with channas and tangy chutneys. It can be made only with potatoes or stuffed with peas or dry daals; sometimes even with raisons. **The variations are unlimited.** A simple snack to make, but requires an expertise and experience to be able keep the tikkis together while frying them.

Recipe; Makes 12-15 tikkis depending on the size

Ingredients

6 medium size potatoes

1/2 cup boiled peas (optional)

1 medium onion, finely chopped

2 green chillis finely chopped

1/2 inch piece ginger, finely grated (optional)

2 tablespoons of fresh chopped coriander

1 teaspoon salt

1/teaspoon red chilli or paprika

1/2 teaspoon garam masaala

2 slices white bread

3 tablespoons of plain flour for coating

Oil for shallow frying

For garnishing;
salad leaves; pinch of chaat masaala; sprigs of coriander; wedges of lemon; slices of onion

Method

(1) Boil the potatoes with the skins on. When soft, take them off the heat, cool them, take the skin off and if using peas, add them at this stage and mash the potatoes and peas together.

(2) Add the onions, chilli, ginger and coriander and mix well. Add the salt and spices, chilli or paprika and garam masaala and mix again.

(3) Wet the bread slices thoroughly; squeeze the water out and mix the bread with the potato mixture well, making sure that there are no lumps of either the potato or the bread.

(4) Grease the palms; Make small flat cakes; a diameter of 2-3 inches with a thickness of 1/2 inch. Make as many as possible, the number depending upon the diameter of the cakes. Dust them lightly with the plain flour; cover with a damp cloth and set them aside.

(5) Heat 3 spoons of oil in a deep frying pan. When sizzling add the potato tikkis one by one, as many as the pan will allow. Allow to cook about two minutes each side; make sure they are golden brown in colour; take them out and set them on a greaseproof paper Keep them warm while finishing making the rest of the tikkis in the same way. Serve warm.

Garnish; on a bed of salad leaves; sprigs of coriander on top; wedges of lemon and slices of onion on the side; sprinkle chaat masaala on top.

Serve; as a snack; as a starter; part of a buffet spread; part of the chaat group of foods with chickpeas and imli chutney.

Overall cooking time: 1 hour.

Mom's Tips

(1) Choose the variety of potato carefully as floury potatoes make better tikkis; the sticky potatoes tend to be too soft and mushy.

(2) Not a good dish to freeze as the cakes will fall apart when defrosted. These can be made 4 to 6 hours earlier, half fried and left to be finished off just before serving.

SHAMMI KEBABS

(Minced Lamb Kebabs)

A snack made with the influence of the north west frontier cuisine, this is popular in the north and the metropolitan cities like Delhi and Mumbai, where it is *served at cocktails; with drinks; or as a starter;* Exotic in taste, shammi kebabs was a party dish as it involved a lengthy process which fascinated me as a child as the grinding was done in a mortal and pestle. The food processor has made this task much easier and the freezers have made the kebabs much more accessible at a short notice.

Recipe; Makes 16-22 kebabs, depending on the size

Ingredients

1kg lean lamb mince

1/2 cup of chane ki daal

1 small onion finely chopped

1 inch cube of ginger, finely chopped

6-8 cloves of garlic finely chopped

1-2 small green chillies finely chopped

2 tablespoons of chopped coriander

1 teaspoon salt

1 teaspoon of garam masaala

1/2 teaspoon of red chillies or paprika

2 tablespoon of plain flour for coating

Oil for frying

For garnishing;

lettuce leaves, wedges of lemon

Methad

(1) Put the mince, the daal and the onion in a saucepan with 4-5 tablespoons of water and set it on a med heat. Bring to boil and simmer for 1/2 hour or until the mince and the daal is cooked and the water has evaporated, leaving it as a dry dish. Leave to cool.

(2) Put the dry dish of the mince and daal into a food processor and process for 2-3 mins or until it looks smooth

(3) Mix the rest of the ingredients in this mixture; ginger, garlic, chilli, coriander, salt, garam masaala and red chillies.

(4) Grease the palms and then make small balls, flatten them slightly, coat each in plain flour and set them on a greased tray.

(5) Fry the kebabs in preheated oil for 2-3 mins on each side or until golden brown keep aside on greaseproof paper till all are done. Serve hot.

Garnish;

arrange the leaves under the kebabs or shred them and put around them; arrange the lemon edges on the side.

Serve;

As a snack or starter. Arrange the salad leaves on a plate; put the kebabs on the leaves; arrange the wedges of lemon on the side and serve with a mint chutney.

Overall cooking time: 1hr 15mins to 1hr 30mins.

Mom's Tips

(1) A very good dish to freeze after step 4. The trays can be put in the freezer so the kebabs can be frozen individually. This makes it easier to take out whatever number is required at a time. You can also half fry the kebabs and keep them on the greaseproof paper and dip them in hot oil just before serving; or finish frying and reheat in the microwave.

(2) It does not take much more effort to make twice the quantity and being a good dish for the freezer it makes it an ideal party dish.

TANDOORI
(Bar-be-cued or Grilled);

Tandoori Murgh
(Spicy Chicken bar-be-cued or grilled)

Mutton Tikke
(Spicy Lamb pieces - grilled)

Seekh Kebabs
(Lamb mince Kebabs - grilled)

Murgh Tikke
(Chicken pieces in spicy marinade - grilled)

Mirch Machhi ke Tikke
(Fish pieces in a chilli marinade - grilled)

Section 2

Traditionally Indian cooking is done on top of a hob, never in a conventional oven; the only exception being, the *'Tandoor'*, which is the Indian barbecue-cum-grill, and occasionally an oven with limitations. By appearance and description, it is a round clay oven. This oven can be anything between 2 ft. - 5 ft., smaller ones found in the patios or yards of private houses, larger ones in restaurants. **It is cylindrical in shape, with a small opening on top, about half the size of the base.** It is mostly embedded in the earth with a side opening just above the level of the ground with a small air hole at the bottom to allow air in when it is heating; which is through the medium of charcoal or wood.

Ideal for cooking marinated meats, chicken, fish or mutton, minced 'kebabs' or diced vegetables. These are threaded onto skewers called 'Seekhs', which are then lowered into the Tandoor on to a wire mesh laid on top of the coals. Apart from the fact that it *uses very little oil or fat*, the cooked result is excellent as the **hot coals sear the outside** of the meats, while retaining the juices inside. Also popular for making 'Rotis' (Indian bread in the shape of a pancake, bland in taste, but superb to have with curries) which can be stuck on the inside walls of the clay ovens which are searing hot; or corn on the cob; sweet potatoes or even ordinary potatoes in their jackets can be lowered onto the hot ashes to cook.

My father was a doctor in the Indian Armed forces and as such was posted to different places

every 2-3 years and one of the first things my mother did was to get a Tandoor made in the back yard of each new house. It gave us a delightful focal point for the whole family with our barbecues of tandoori meats and various types of rotis filled with chopped onion, grated cauliflower or mashed potato; in the winter to enjoy the afternoon sun, in the summer the cool evening breeze.

When the main cooking was done, my mother would beat a Victorian sponge cake mixture, put it into a tin, lower it into the Tandoor and cover the oven with a metallic tray for an hour or so. Then we had the most perfectly baked cake with a smell of the fresh air and coal that I have never since had in all my years of baking in a conventional oven. My mother never knew about oven temperature; she worked by instinct.

Electric grills can be used in rainy days, gas barbecues can be lit for convenience, but we have found the coal barbecues to come the closest in the smell to the original Tandoor although the smell of the clay still remains missing.

Traditionally the term 'Tikka' or 'Tikke' in the plural was used for a small pieces of meat cooked in the Tandoor as apposed to a 'Kebab' which was made from Minced Meat, Fish, or even Paneer. These were shaped round or cylindrical, if grilled they were shaped on a skewer. Generally deep fried like Shammi Kebab or Reshmi Kebab. Now these terms seem to be interchanging.

TANDOORI MURGH

(Spicy Chicken - bar-be-cued or grilled)

The term *Tandoori Murg* is derived from the word **'Tandoor'**. To put simply, it implies chicken, since Murg means chicken, cooked and grilled in a clay oven called the 'Tandoor'. Since Tandoors are now not available or practical, the **marinaded chicken can be cooked either in a hot oven or under a pre-heated grill**. Also, since Tandoors would cook small whole chickens evenly, and grills or barbecues don't, it is better to use chicken pieces in the grill. Of these, legs and thighs or whole drumsticks absorb the marinade flavours better as they are stronger meat than the breast pieces, although either can be used. *A great party dish,* it can be served as it is barbecued, or made into a more exotic dish in which it is smothered in a rich butter-tomato sauce. See recipe for Murg Makhani

Recipe; Serves 4

Ingredients

8 pieces of chicken (counting leg and thigh as two pieces)

Marinade;

1 inch cube of ginger, roughly chopped

3 cloves of garlic, roughly chopped

1 small green chilli, finely chopped

2 tablespoons chopped coriander

2-3 three tablespoons of natural yoghurt

1 teaspoon of tomato puree (optional)

1 teaspoon of vinegar

1 teaspoon of lemon juice

1 teaspoon of paprika

1/2 teaspoon of red chillies

1/2 teaspoon of garam masaala

1/2 teaspoon of orange food colouring (optional)

1 teaspoon of salt

1 tablespoon of cooking oil

For garnishing;

slices of raw onion, lemon wedges and a pinch of amchur, salt and garam masaala.

Method

(1) First prepare the chicken. Skin the chicken pieces and make two cuts in each piece at an angle to the bone. Set them aside.

(2) Make a paste of the ginger, garlic, chilli and fresh coriander. This can be done in a food processor or in a mortar and pestle. Mix this with the rest of the marinade ingredients including the cooking oil.

(3) Put the chicken pieces in the marinade, mix well, making sure that each piece is covered with the marinade; cover and set aside for at least 4-5 hours or overnight in the fridge.

(4) Pre-set the grill to the highest setting. When hot, place the chicken pieces on the wire rack and grill them. It should take 30 mins to cook; 15 mins each side. Brush with the marinade or oil once on each side. If necessary reduce the heat after 15 mins. If cooking in a hot oven, it may take about 40 mins, but remember to turn the pieces once in the oven also. When you take the pieces out, **check to make sure the chicken is cooked through;** garnish and serve, hot or cold.

Garnish:

Sprinkle salt, garam masaala and amchur, and garnish with wedges of lemon or squeeze the juice of half of lemon on the chicken pieces. Add a sprig of coriander on top.

Serve;

With onion rice or pooris or chapaatis, and a lentil or a curry dish, and yoghurt on the side; it is equally delightful with garlic bread, a coleslaw and green salad.

Overall Cooking Time:

20 mins to marinade and 30 mins to cook.

Mom's Tips

(1) Always skin the chicken before marinading to allow the flavours to Permeate the flesh.

(2) The cuts in the chicken are important for the marinade to soak. The **cuts must always be on an angle to the bone,** never parallel to it, or the flesh will fall off when cooking.

(3) A bit of the cooking oil is important to add in the marinade as it keeps the chicken moist while cooking, but if you are cutting down the fat, the oil can be omitted.

(4) *You can substitute the paprika, red chillies, garam masaala and the food colouring for two teaspoons of tandoori masaala,* and then reduce the quantity of salt to half a teaspoon.

(5) If there is any thick sauce left below the grill or in the roasting pan, serve in a small dish along with the chicken.

(6) It can be cooked in advance, arranged on a tray and heated in a micro- wave oven. This dish is also ideal for freezing, either after the marinade stage or when fully cooked. It can be reheated in the microwave or under the grill.

MUTTON TIKKE

(Spicy Lamb pieces – grilled)

A North Indian dish, popular in the winter when there are street vendors with their hot clay ovens, on the roadside, with their platters of marinaded meats, warming themselves beside the heat, till the customers came; the flurry of activity then started; the skewers went on the coals; the banana leaves came out as disposable plates; the tandoori aroma wafted around; these are the memories of childhood. A dish all the more special at that time as in India it is generally goat meat instead of lamb which is tougher and therefore has to be marinaded for at least 24 hours in a meat tenderizer for the pieces to be cooked through on a high heat in just a few mins; and Tandoors were not part of every household **Now with lamb it has become a more accessible dish; and barbecues and grills have made it an easier dish to make; a versatile dish as it can be added to an Indian meal or a western barbecue.**

Recipe; serves 4-6 people.

Ingredients

1kg of lamb leg meat, boned, cut into 1 inch cube pieces

2-3 small onions quartered, optional

Marinade

1 inch cube ginger finely chopped

5-6 cloves of garlic finely chopped

1 green chilli finely chopped

2 tablespoon chopped fresh coriander

1 teaspoon of ground coriander seeds

1 teaspoon of ground cumin seeds

1/2 teaspoon of red chilli

1/2 teaspoon of garam masaala

10-12 peppercorns crushed

1/4 teaspoon ground nutmeg

1/2 teaspoon salt

2 tablespoon lemon juice

2 tablespoons oil

Skewers;   6 to 8

For garnishing;

wedges of lemon, spring onions and fresh bay leaves

Method

(1) Trim the lamb of any excess fat. Wash and set aside

(2) Make the marinade; add all the ingredient fresh, ground, liquid's; ginger, garlic, chilli, coriander, red chilli, garam masaala, peppercorns, nutmeg, salt, lemon juice, oil. Mix well.

(3) Put the meat pieces in the marinade and mix thoroughly making sure all the pieces are coated. Cover and set aside for 3-4 hrs, mixing occasionally.

(4) Skewer the kebabs, interspersing with as much onion as you want or none at all. Heat the barbecue or the grill and cook the meat on the skewers for 10-12 mins or until the meat is cooked as desired. Garnish and serve hot.

Garnish;
arrange wedges of lemon spring onions and bay leaves.

Serve; with a mint or tomato chutney as a starter or with cocktails; rolled up in a chapaathi as a snack with any other barbecued meat, baked potato and green salad; with any Indian meal.

Overall cooking time: Preparation time 25-30 mins, cooking time 12-15 mins

Variation

If you want to add vegetables, reduce the quantity of meat and add sliced courgettes & peppers in the same marinade and intersperse them with the meat.

Mom's Tips

(1) To be prepared early, *you can marinade the night before* and keep the meat in the refrigerator; take it out an hour before cooking to arrive at room temperature.

(2) **Oil is important in the marinade** otherwise the meat will be dry and tough.

(3) **Not a good dish to freeze**

SEEKH KEBABS

(Lamb mince Kebabs - grilled)

An interesting tandoori dish, originally from the North west of India, it is now very popular in the west with its variations. *A casual dish, it can be had for a light lunch with just a green salad and a garlic bread; it can be a snack with cocktails; or be part of a full supper menu.* In Delhi it is a very popular sight to see road side vendors making these kebabs on hot coals, on a cold winter's evening, and the shoppers would be eating them out of old newspapers making the outing a lot more interesting especially for children. **Traditionally these kebabs are made with lamb mince because that is the meat used in India but you can substitute it for beef mince if you so prefer.**

Recipe; Makes 6-8 kebabs (depending on the size)

Ingredients; Method

3/4 kg of lean lamb mince

1 small onion, finely chopped (optional)

1 inch cube of ginger

6-7 cloves of garlic

1-2 small green chillies

6-7 sprigs of fresh coriander

10-12 peppercorns, coarsely crushed

1/2 teaspoon of ground roasted cummin seeds

1 teaspoon of garam masaala

1/2 teaspoon of red chillies (optional)

1 teaspoon of salt

1 egg, lightly beaten

1 tablespoon of oil

A few salad leaves

8-10 skewer

For garnishing; 2-3 sprigs of coriander, chopped, wedges of lemon, a few salad leaves

(1) First prepare the masaala paste. Either grind the ginger, cloves of garlic, chilli and fresh coriander in a mortar pestle or process them in a food processor and set them aside.

(2) Put the mince in a bowl, mix in the onion and the above paste and mix well. Now add the dry spices, crushed peppercorns, roasted cumin seed, garam masaala, red chillies and salt and again mix well. Add the egg little by little and keep mixing till all the egg is incorporated and the mixture is still firm enough to hold together.

(3) Divide the mixture into as many portions as you want to make the kebabs. Generally I divide it into 8-10 portions. Then oil the palm of your hands and working with your hands shape each portion of the mixture round each skewer to a length of about 3-4 inches.

(4) If you want to make them on a barbecue arrange them on it and it should take about 10-12 mins to cook them. Keep rotating them. If making them in the grill, preheat to the highest setting and it should take the same amount of time, brushing with a little oil if necessary. Arrange them on top of salad leaves in a shallow dish, garnish and serve hot.

Garnish; sprinkle chopped fresh coriander; arrange the lemon wedges on the side of the plate so that a bit of lemon juice can be sprinkled on the kebab when serving.

Serve; With a coleslaw and a garlic bread for lunch; as a snack with drinks; as a dish in a supper menu; or even as a starter.

Overall cooking time: 30 to 40 mins.

Mom's Tips

(1) **Make sure the utensils are dry** before you start because the mixture should be as firm as possible for it to stay round the skewer. For the same reason Try and get fresh mince instead of frozen as the frozen will be wetter when it defrosts.

(2) **Make sure the mince is lean** as fatty mince will lose its shape and bulk when cooking, apart from the fact that it does not taste as nice as the lean mince does.

(3) If adding the onion it must be very finely chopped, or the meat might not hold very well. For the same reason, if you do not have a food processor or a mortar pestle for the masaala paste, chop all the ingredients very finely.

(3) These kebabs are very good for freezing; they can be frozen either after step three, after shaping them onto the skewers and then cooked after defrosting them; or after they have been cooked, in which case you would only need to reheat them.

MURGH TIKKE

(Chicken pieces in spicy marinade - grilled)

A North Indian tandoori dish, it has become very popular in the west for their barbecues and grills; infact it has become part of their summer cuisine. A *very versatile dish*, it is equally delightful with garlic bread and a green salad as it is with tandoori roti or a rice pulao; the tikkas can me made on their own; they can be interspersed with vegetables; or they can have a *masaala* sauce poured over them and be called by the well known name of *Tikka masaala*.

Recipe; Serves 4

Ingredients

4 chicken breast fillets, skinned and boned

1 green pepper, cut into inch square pieces

1 red or yellow pepper, cut into inch square pieces

4 large tomatoes, quartered, or 8 medium tomatoes halved

1 medium sized onion, cut into inch square pieces

12 small mushrooms, washed and trimmed

Marinade
for the chicken, peppers, mushrooms;

1 inch cube of ginger, roughly chopped

6 cloves of garlic, roughly chopped

1 green chilli, chopped

3 tablespoons of fresh chopped coriander

3 tablespoon of natural yoghurt

2 tablespoon of cooking oil

1 tablespoon of lemon juice

2 teaspoons of tandoori masaala

1/2 teaspoon of garam masaala

1/2 teaspoon of salt

Marinade *for the onions, tomatoes;*

2 cloves of garlic, finely chopped

2 sprigs of fresh coriander, finely chopped

1 tablespoon of cooking oil

1 tablespoon of lemon juice

Pinch of garam masaala

Pinch of salt

For garnishing;
4 sprigs of fresh coriander or parsley, chopped, 3-4 wedges of lemon

Method

(1) First prepare the chicken; take a sharp knife and cut strips of chicken, not too small, about an inch wide and three inches long. You should get about four pieces to a fillet. Set them aside.

(2) Put the cut vegetables into small bowls separately and set them aside.

(3) To make the marinade; put the ginger, garlic, chilli and fresh coriander into a mortar and pestle and make a paste; Alternatively put the ingredients into a food processor and finely chop them. Add the yoghurt, oil, lemon juice, tandoori masaala, garam masaala and salt and mix well.

(4) Put the chicken strips in half of the marinade; mix well till each piece is well coated. Cover and set aside for 3-4 hours.

(5) When ready to cook, take the other half of the marinade and coat the peppers and the mushrooms. Mix the chopped garlic, fresh coriander, cooking oil, lemon juice, garam masaala and salt in a dish and coat the onions amid tomatoes with this marinade.

(6) Set the grill on to full heat.

(7) Now take 4 large or 6 small skewers and put the chicken and vegetables on them in any order you like, as long as you start with an onion and finish with an onion as that holds all the pieces in place. When putting the chicken pieces on, put each piece on the skewer from both ends, as that then prevents the pieces from falling off. Set these on the wire mesh of a grill pan.

(8) Set the grill pan with the skewers on top under the hot grill and cook about 4-6 mins; Then rotate the skewers and cook for another 4-6 mins. They should be brown on the outside. Take them out, check that they are cooked; garnish and serve them. They can be served on the skewers; or taken off the skewers and served in a flat dish.

Garnish;

sprinkle chopped fresh coriander; arrange wedges of lemon.

Serve;

With tandoori roti or pooris, and a yoghurt dish; or a rice pulao and a daal with a raita; it can also be served with a jacket potato, a green salad, and garlic bread; any Indian meal

Overall cooking time:

1/2 hour for marinade and 10 -15mins to cook .

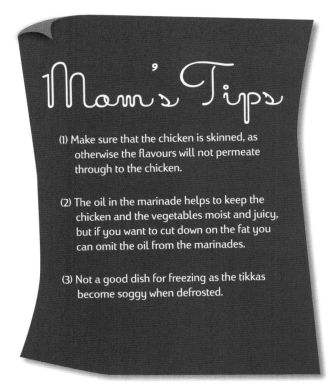

Mom's Tips

(1) Make sure that the chicken is skinned, as otherwise the flavours will not permeate through to the chicken.

(2) The oil in the marinade helps to keep the chicken and the vegetables moist and juicy, but if you want to cut down on the fat you can omit the oil from the marinades.

(3) Not a good dish for freezing as the tikkas become soggy when defrosted.

MIRCH MACHHI KE TIKKE

(Fish pieces in a chilli marinade - grilled)

A spicy dish; a variation of the north Indian style of barbecue cooking with fish; and the chilli is to spice the soft taste of fish. *Since fish is soft in texture as well this dish is best made with a firm fish like the hake or monkfish tails which will not fall apart when working with the skewers.* Very popular in the Delhi and Panjab regions in the winter as the street vendors will try to cater for all styles and tastes in their marinated cuisine from mild to hot; eating it out of the cones made with banana leaves with spicy chutneys is an unforgettable experience; **again a versatile dish** as it can be served at any time of the day, as a snack or starter with a main meal.

Recipe; Serves 4-5 people

Ingredients

3/4 kg fish, hake, monkfish tails or any fish cut into 2 inch cubes

1 tablespoon of lemon juice

1/2 teaspoon salt

1/2 teaspoon garam masaala

10-12 small cherry tomatoes

Marinade;

1 inch cube of ginger finely chopped

1 green chilli finely chopped

1 tablespoon of chopped fresh coriander

1 teaspoon of ground coriander seeds

1 teaspoon of ground cumin seeds

1/2 teaspoon of red chilli or paprika

1/4 teaspoon of garam masaala

1/4 teaspoon salt

1 tablespoon of garlic vinegar

1 tablespoon of oil

Skewers; 5-6

For garnishing;

chopped coriander, wedges of lemon, cherry tomatoes, fresh green chillies

Method

(1) Wash the fish cubes and drain well. Rub in the lemon juice, salt and garam masaala and set aside for 2 hours or while preparing the marinade.

(2) Add all the marinading ingredients together; ginger, chilli, fresh coriander, ground coriander, cumin, red chilli, garam masaala, salt, garlic vinegar, oil and mix well. Add to the fish and coat all the pieces thoroughly. Cover and set aside for 2-3 hrs.

(3) Skewer the fish pieces and intersperse with small round tomatoes if using them. Heat the barbecue or the grill and cook them for 4-5 mins, or until done, turning them occasionally. Garnish and serve hot.

Garnish;

sprinkle coriander over the kebabs, place lemon wedges and halved cherry tomatoes on the side and fresh green chillies.

Serve;

as a starter or as a cocktail snack with mint with yoghurt chutney; or as a side dish with any western barbecue or an Indian meal.

Overall cooking time:

20 mins preparation and 10 mins cooking time

Mom's Tips

(1) **The first step is important as it takes away the fishy smell** and firms the texture for the barbecue.

(2) *Not a good dish to freeze.*

MAAS

(Meat);

Rogan Josh
(Lamb Meat curry)

Keema Matar
(Mince and Pea curry)

Raan Masaaledar
(Spiced roast Leg of Lamb)

Saag Meat
(Meat with Spinach)

Meat Korma
(Lamb Meat curry with yoghurt)

Section 3

In non-vegetarian Indian cooking, **meat is very popular, particularly lamb meat**. It is cooked in all forms, dry; curried, or roasted; it can be made on its own, with vegetables, or added to rice dishes called Biryaanis; available in the most expensive of restaurants, or in the cheapest of roadside cafes in India called 'Dhaabas'. The only difference between India and Britain is that in India we use goat meat, in Britain we use lamb; leaving the dish with a much stronger flavour in India. When I have relatives over from India they find the meat, or for that matter chicken, much more bland here, but then on the other hand, my Irish friends who have visited India with me have found it very difficult to get used to the strong meat flavour there.

In India meat is asked for, and sold just by weight, and not by specific portions. So the butcher puts in a bit of all portions, unless you are specific. When I first came to Northern Ireland and went into a butcher's shop, the different portions of a lamb, or for that matter beef , even their pictures on the wall, totally confused me. I experimented and learnt as I went along. I personally like a leg of lamb for most of my dishes and if you have a good butcher he will cut it up for you in inch cube pieces. He may not initially like to do it as he may consider it a sacrilege to cut up a good Sunday roast, as mine did, but he will get used to it. To give it extra flavour, add a small shank or few pieces of the neck and shoulder. Make sure the butcher also *trims off the excess fat*, as, apart from health reasons, fat may be necessary in oven cooking but not in making curries. In India the butchers have there art of taking fat off every piece to perfection, which is fascinating to watch, difficult to practice.

Some dishes are also made with rib cutlets and chops, I will specifically mention that in those recipes.

The meat is always cut with the bone in India, because the bone affects the taste and texture of the curry. Infact as children we always fought for the marrow bone from which the marrow was scooped out with a thin long spoon which was set on the table specifically for such a purpose. If for the sake of convenience you decide to make these curries with boned meat then, if possible put in the whole cleaned bone while making the curry and then discard it before serving the dish.

I find that better cuts of lamb make better curries. When making mince curry I tend to use lamb mince and as it is generally not available I tend to buy a lean cut and ask my butcher to mince it for me as it does work economical as well in the long run; apart from the taste, less fat will mean more meat. Years ago I came across a colleague who would buy and freeze half a lamb, roast the better portions and then ask me for curry recipes to use up the cheaper cuts believing that spices would mask their flavour. This is erroneous. **Spices do not mask, they** *enhance* **flavours.** Good cuts of meat will make good flavoured curries, vice versa, and you may not want to experiment again.

The above discussion is more on lamb since, as mentioned elsewhere, beef is generally not eaten in India, while pork is eaten, but on a much smaller scale. If you prefer, you can substitute beef pieces or pork pieces, although chopping the bone with these meats is not practical, but take care to get the good portions in both meats and have the excess fat trimmed. Personally, I think that lamb meat absorbs the spice flavours the best, but then I could be biased

ROGAN JOSH (Lamb Meat curry);

This is the most popular of Indian meat dishes, on the menu of every restaurant that I have ever visited in India or Britain. **It is a mild curry**, authentic, easy to make and a good starting place for a novice to start experimenting with Indian cooking. **Try to get the meat chopped with the bone**; otherwise it can be made with lamb pieces also. A firm favourite with children, I have found that this dish can be made more interesting for them by adding diced potatoes or new whole potatoes to the dish, 20 mins before the end of cooking time.

Recipe; Serves 4-5

Ingredients

1 kg lamb meat (preferably leg meat cut into one inch cubes with the bone)

1 black cardamom, split

2-3 cloves

1 stick of cinnamon, an inch long

3 bay leaves

1 large onion, finely chopped

1 inch cube of ginger, chopped

4 cloves of garlic, chopped

2 fresh tomatoes chopped, or a small can of chopped tomatoes

1 green chilli, chopped

1 teaspoon of ground coriander seeds

1 teaspoon of ground cumin seeds

1 teaspoon of ground fenugreek seeds

1/2 teaspoon of paprika

1/2 teaspoon of red chillies (optional)

1/2 teaspoon of garam masaala

1/2 teaspoon of turmeric

1 teaspoons of salt

2 glasses of water or stock

3 tablespoons of oil

For garnishing; 4 sprigs of fresh coriander or parsley, chopped, and a pinch of garam masaala

Method

(1) Put the oil in a heavy based pan and heat on medium heat. Fry the cardamom, cloves, cinnamon and bay leaves for 1 min.

(2) Add the onion, garlic, ginger and brown them to make the masaala. This will take 3-5 mins.

(3) Put the tomato, fresh or canned, and the green chilli in, and fry for 2-3 mins.

(4) Add the dry spices; coriander, cumin, fenugreek, paprika, red chillies, garam masaala and turmeric to the above, and fry for 1-2 mins.

(5) Add the meat and salt and mix it well. Cover and leave for a few mins. Stirring occasionally.

(6) Dry the juices of the meat till the oil begins to show. Roast the meat in the oil and masaala for 2-3 mins mixing frequently. Should take 20-25 mins.

(7) Put in 2 glasses of water, cover and simmer on low heat until tender, about 25-30 mins. Check the thickness of the gravy, taste the salt; garnish and serve hot.

Garnish;
with chopped coriander or parsley and sprinkle a pinch of garam masaala

Serve;
with boiled rice or onion pulao, a yoghurt and a green salad; or chapaathis or pooris, with a dry vegetable dish or a dry daal and a raita.

Overall Cooking Time: 1 hour.

Mom's Tips

(1) Depending on how tomatoey you would like your curry to be, you could **reduce or increase the amount of tomato.**

(2) make sure *the butcher trims off excess fat* from the meat pieces, Fat is essential when roasting in the oven not when making a curry.

(3) If the meat gives out too much of the juices in step (5), dry the meat on a high heat. Also, check the thickness of the sauce just before serving; if it is too thick add a few tablespoons of boiling water, if too thin, dry on a high heat, stirring constantly so that it does not stick to the bottom of the pan.

(4) An ideal dish for freezing. Make small packs and defrost as many as required. Reheat in the microwave.

KEEMA MATAR

(Mince and Pea curry);

Basically a North Indian dish, this was top of the list of the favourites of the girls in my cooking classes as it is cost effective when buying the ingredients and a time saver to make. **It is a mild dish, yet gives the aroma of herbs and spices;** its versatility is brilliant as it can be accompanied by rice, roti, naan, garlic bread, even boiled potato.
I would generally use lamb mince; it is now readily available in some big chain stores, otherwise you could ask your butcher to make you some; but if you prefer, **you could make this dish with beef mince with just as much success.**

Recipe; Serves 5-6

Ingredients

1kg. of mince, lamb or beef

1 cup of fresh or frozen peas

1 black cardamom, split

1 large onion, finely chopped

1 inch cube of ginger, finely chopped

4-5 cloves of garlic, finely chopped

2 medium sized tomatoes, chopped, or a small can of chopped tomatoes

2 small green chillies, finely chopped

1 teaspoon of ground coriander seeds

1 teaspoon of ground cumin seed

1/2 teaspoon of paprika

1/2 teaspoon of red chillies

1/2 teaspoon of garam masaala

1/2 teaspoon of turmeric

1 teaspoon of salt

1 1/2 glasses of water or stock

3 tablespoons of oil

For garnishing; 5-6 sprigs of fresh coriander or parsley, chopped, and pinch of garam masaala

Method

(1) Heat the oil on medium heat in a broad heavy based pan and fry the cardamom for 1/2 min. Add the onion, ginger, and garlic and fry them till they are golden brown. This should take about 4-5 mins

(2) Add the chopped tomato or the can of tomatoes and fry for 1-2 mins.

(3) Add the dry spices, coriander, cumin, paprika, red chillies, garam masaala, and turmeric and fry for one min.

(4) Put in the mince and mix well. Cover the pan and let it cook in its own juices for 10-15 mins or till it is dry. Stir it well and roast it in the oil for 4-5 mins.

(5) Add 1 1/2 glasses of water or stock, bring it to the boil, and let it simmer for 15 mins. Then add the peas, leave it on for another 15 mins making it a total of 40 mins, switch off the heat, taste the salt, garnish and serve hot.

Garnish;
sprinkle a pinch of garam masaala; arrange chopped coriander or parsley

Serve;
As a main dish, with rice, boiled or onion pulao, chapaati, naan or even plain bread; a green salad and yoghurt dish.

Overall cooking time: 1 hour

Mom's Tips

(1) the most important point is this dish is to **make sure the mince is lean** otherwise, as apart from losing its bulk during cooking, fatty mince makes the dish very greasy and gives it a poor taste. If there is excess fat at the end of cooking, drain it off before serving.

(2) Sometimes lamb can give out a lot of juices, especially the spring lamb; so keep a watch on the cooking time scale, put the heat high if required and reduce the measure of water if necessary.

(3) If you are using fresh peas put them in 20 mins. before the end of cooking time. *If using frozen peas put them in as above if the dish is to be served immediately or the peas lose their fresh green colour.* If you are going to freeze the dish then add the peas when the dish is thawed out as the peas will cook as the dish is reheating.

(4) An excellent dish to freeze. It can be thawed easily and reheated in the microwave or the hob.

RAAN MASAALEDAR

(Spiced roast leg of Lamb);

Making any meat or chicken curried dish in a large quantity on a domestic hob particularly an electric one is challenging and daunting as these dishes are made by roasting the meat or chicken in the onion and spice masaala and the danger is of the bottom layer sticking to the pan and the dish having a burnt flavour of overdone meat. So I experimented with spices and whole pieces of meat in the oven and the roast leg was the most successful. If I have a larger crowd to entertain I just have to double the quantity of spices and put two joints in the oven instead of one.

Recipe; serves 8 people

Ingredients

1 1/2 kg leg of lamb

For marinade,

7-8 cloves

2 inches long stick of cinnamon

2 deseeded black cardamoms

10-15 black peppercorns

1 cup of natural yoghurt (home made or commercial)

2 inch cube of ginger finely chopped

8-10 cloves of garlic finely chopped

1-2 green chillies finely chopped

2 tablespoons of fresh chopped coriander

1 tablespoon of ground coriander

1 teaspoon of red chillies

1 teaspoon of garam masaala

4 bay leaves

1 teaspoon of salt

1 tablespoon of lemon juice

2 tablespoons of oil

For garnishing;

5-6 cloves, teaspoon of yoghurt and chopped coriander

Method

(1) Wash the leg of lamb. Prepare by making shallow incisions in the lamb to allow the marinade to soak in its flavors. Set aside.

(2) Put the cloves, cinnamon, cardamoms and peppercorns in a grinder and coarsely grind them

(3) **Prepare the marinade.** Put all the rest of the ingredients in the natural yoghurt; ginger, garlic, chilli, fresh coriander, coarsely ground spices, bay leaves, lemon juice and oil; mix well. Coat the leg of lamb well with it and leave for 6-8 hrs or overnight in the fridge.

(4) Take the lamb out of the fridge 1 hour before cooking. Place it in a roasting dish and cover it with foil.

(5) Preheat the oven to 170 C. (150 C for a fan oven). When it is heated, place the covered lamb in the centre shelf and give it a cooking time of 20 mins to the pound and an extra 20 mins. Halfway through the cooking check with the skewer and adjust the time accordingly; uncover the joint 15 mins before the end of cooking. When the meat is cooked, take it out of the oven and leave it sitting for 10 mins. Arrange the joint on a platter; pour the curried juices over it; garnish and serve.

Garnish;
spoon the tablespoon of yoghurt and arrange the cloves and the sprig of coriander on the joint

Serve;
Slices of meat with a spoon of the curry on it; with rice and a garlic bread or with jacket potatoes and spiced cabbage.

Overall cooking time:- 15 mins to marinade. Oven cooking time will depend on the weight of the joint.

Mom's Tips

(1) You can use **whole peppercorns,** *but they can be crunchy and spicy* when bitten into, therefore I prefer to crush them.

(2) If the curried **juices look too much put them in a saucepan and boil them down** until they achieve a consistency that you like.

(3) **A good dish to freeze.** Slice the meat, arrange on a serving tray, pour the juices over it and freeze.

SAAG MEAT  (Meat with Spinach);

Adding vegetables or lentils to meat or chicken dishes is an age old tradition in Indian cooking. Three reasons; it is a cost effective way to increase the volume of a dish while retaining the taste; in a generally hot country, climate wise, these additions reduces the intake of meat; this style eliminates the need of a separate vegetable dish. Spinach is particularly interesting to add, as apart from being of high nutritional value it absorbs the spices and flavour of meat well as it is otherwise a bland vegetable on its own. This particularly is a favourite dish of my family.

Recipe; Serves 5-6

Ingredients

1kg of lamb meat, diced with the bone, or beef pieces

500 g. of fresh, chopped spinach, or one packet of cut leaf frozen spinach

2 small green cardamoms

1 large onion, chopped

1 piece of ginger, an inch cube, chopped

4-5 cloves of garlic, chopped

2 medium sized fresh tomatoes, chopped or a small can of tomatoes

2 tablespoons of natural yoghurt

1 green chilli, chopped,

1 teaspoon of ground coriander seeds

1 teaspoon of ground cumin seeds

1 teaspoon of ground fenugreek seeds

1/2 teaspoon of paprika

1/2 teaspoon of red chilli

1 teaspoon of garam masaala

1 teaspoon of turmeric

1 teaspoon of salt

1 1/2 glasses of water or stock

3-4 tablespoons of cooking oil

For garnishing; 1 teaspoon of double cream, few fried onion rings or thinly sliced tomato

Method

(1) Heat the oil in a heavy based pan, on medium heat and fry the cardamoms for 1 min.

(2) Put in the onion, ginger, garlic, and chillies and brown to make the masaala.

(3) Add the tomatoes, yoghurt and green chilli and fry for 3-4 mins.

(4) Add the dry spices; coriander, cumin, fenugreek, paprika, red chillies, garam masaala and turmeric. Fry for 1-2 mins.

(5) Add the meat and salt mix well, cover the pan and leave on a medium heat. Stir periodically, and try to dry the juices of the meat and roast the meat dry. This should take 15-20 mins.

(6) Add the spinach and roast for another 10 mins.

(7) Put in 1 1/2 glasses of water or lamb stock. Simmer for another 25-30 mins or until the lamb is tender. Check the consistency of the gravy, taste the salt; garnish and serve hot.

Garnish; spoon the cream in the centre of the dish, arrange the onion rings or tomato slices around it.

Serve; With a chapatti, naan, or boiled rice, a yoghurt dish and dry lentil with a side salad of chopped onion, tomato and cucumber called 'Kachumbhar' salad.

Overall cooking time: 1hr to 1hr and 10 mins.

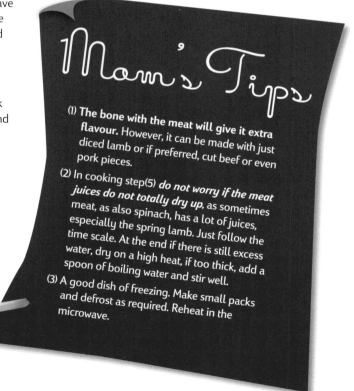

Mom's Tips

(1) **The bone with the meat will give it extra flavour.** However, it can be made with just diced lamb or if preferred, cut beef or even pork pieces.

(2) In cooking step(5) *do not worry if the meat juices do not totally dry up*, as sometimes meat, as also spinach, has a lot of juices, especially the spring lamb. Just follow the time scale. At the end if there is still excess water, dry on a high heat, if too thick, add a spoon of boiling water and stir well.

(3) A good dish of freezing. Make small packs and defrost as required. Reheat in the microwave.

MEAT KORMA

(Lamb Meat curry with yoghurt);

A rich meat dish of Northern India; **traditionally termed as a Mughlai dish,** it has become very popular in the west especially since the chain stores have brought this in their line of Indian dishes. The home-made version, of course would be far nicer than anything made on a commercial basis. Made as mild as you want it or as hot as you want, it is one of those complete dishes; a meal in itself, without the need for accompanying side dishes; which are delicious with either just a naan bread or pulao rice. Originally made with cream, it was a very rich dish. I have tempered it down and substituted yoghurt for cream, making it a lighter version.

Recipe; Serves 5-6

Ingredients

1kg lamb meat, preferably leg or shoulder, cut into 1 1/2 inch pieces with the bone

2 black cardamoms split

4-5 cloves

1 1/2 inch piece of cinnamon

4-5 bay leaves, crushed

8-10 peppercorns, coarsely crushed

1 medium sized onion, peeled

5-6 cloves of garlic, peeled

1 inch cube of ginger

1-2 small green chillies

1/2 tomato, chopped

1 teaspoon of coriander seeds

1 teaspoon of cumin seeds

1 teaspoon of fenugreek seeds

1/2 teaspoon of red chillies

1/2 teaspoon of paprika

1/2 teaspoon of garam masaala

1 teaspoon of turmeric

1 teaspoon of salt

3 tablespoons of yoghurt

1 teaspoon of cream (optional)

1 1/2 glasses of water

4-5 tablespoons of oil

For garnishing; 6-7 sprigs of fresh chopped coriander, 2 red chillies for colour (optional)

Method

(1) First prepare the onion masaala. Put the onion, ginger, garlic and green chillies in the food processor and process them, or chop them very finely.

(2) Heat the oil on a medium heat in a broad heavy based pan. Fry the cardamoms, cloves cinnamon, bay leaf and peppercorns for 30 secs. Add the onion masaala and fry until golden brown. This should take about 4-5 mins. Add the chopped tomato and fry for 1 min.

(3) Add the dry masaalas, coriander, cumin, fenugreek, red chillies, paprika, garam masaala **and** turmeric and fry for 30 secs.

(4) Start to add the yoghurt; one teaspoon at a time, fry it and make sure that it is totally absorbed before adding the next spoonful, until all the yoghurt has been added in.

(5 Put in the meat and the salt and mix well. Let it cook uncovered for about 10-15 mins. Stir often and make sure that the meat juices dry up. Then fry for another couple of minutes till the oil begins to show. Now add the water, bring to the boil, reduce the heat, cover the pan and let it simmer for another 30-35 mins or until the meat is as tender as you like. Switch off the heat and let the pan sit on the hob to finish cooking for about 10 mins. Open the pan and see, if there is too much oil on top, spoon it off now add the cream and heat, check the thickness of the gravy, if too thick you can add a couple of tablespoons of boiling water. Taste the salt, garnish and serve hot.

Garnish;
With chopped coriander; arrange the red chillies

Serve;
With naan or tandoori roti, a side vegetable and an onion tomato salad; or with pulao rice a green salad and a yoghurt dish.

Overall cooking time: 1 hour

Mom's Tips

(1 **Apart from being traditional, I think that the bone chopped up with the meat gives the dish a better flavour,** but if you are not able to get this done, or if you prefer the korma without the bone, then you can make it with only meat pieces.

(2) It is difficult to make an Indian curry without oil because the masaalas need to be fried but if there is oil on top of the dish then draining it will not affect the taste of the dish.

(3) A good dish to freeze. Make small batches so that you can defrost as many as you need. Reheat in the microwave, hob or oven.

Bindis and Bangles

The world is getting smaller; multi cuisines are the norm; inter-racial marriages are on the upward swing; traditions of different countries are getting intermingled. Western dresses are being worn in India; saris are in the news in Britain; jeans are to be found in the Middle East; henna tattoos are the rage in the west. And then we come to the *Bindis and the Bangles* - two of the most delightful of those mystical Eastern traditions that have a magical quality about them. Feminine to the core, they can be worn by the rich and the poor, the busy and the idle, and they will make each one feel special.

First the *Bindis. The Bindi is a coloured dot, put in the centre of the forehead, nearer the eyebrows. It can be anything up to half an inch in diameter.* Centuries ago this dot started as a marriage ritual, infact as part of the wedding ceremony itself. After the marriage vows, the Pundit (Priest) finalized the solemn occasion by witnessing the groom apply this dot or the Bindi on his bride's forehead with a red vermillion powder, which was also put in the parting of the hair called *'Sindoor'*. My first memory of this is at my uncle's wedding when I was ten years old. I was totally mesmerised. The day after the wedding I stole into my aunt's room, and applied the powder as I had seen my aunt do that morning. Needless to say there was a furore in the house, that my grandmother was not pleased would be an understatement, and no-one rested till my face and hair were washed.

Then, **these two marks were the prerogative of the married woman only,** applied freshly every morning as part of the makeup. Apart from a sense of pride, the woman had a visible evidence of marriage, which in the context of the Indian culture, especially in the years gone by, was very important. They were as sacred as a gold band is, as a symbol of marriage, in the west. The difference is that, if the woman became a widow, then by social norms she was not allowed to use the powder again, while in the west, the wedding band can be worn by the woman even after her husband' death.

Then about 20-30 years ago a gradual change took place in society whereby the powder became available in different colours and all girls and women, married, unmarried or widows could use it in bindis to suit the colour of their dress. The powder was then replaced by little coloured dots which had a glue like substance on the back and now could be stuck on the forehead with little effort. This was a boon for countries which have rain all year round, since the powder can run down the face, as I found to my cost when I first came to N. Ireland in 1972

The *Sindoor*, in the parting of the hair, **is still very much a conventional and sacred tradition and has not been tampered with.** It is still red in colour and not used by anyone else but a married woman. Again very difficult to use when in N. Ireland due to its incessant rain, so I have taken to wearing a golden band as an extra symbol of a married woman.

The modern Bindi is in different colours, sizes and shapes. They come as circles, diamonds, stars, hexagons and flowers; they come with shining

glossy exteriors, with a matt finish, or with beads on it. Imagination has run riot in their designing, but each one has the effect of giving an extra glow, an extra lift to the face.

And then there are **Bangles.** It evokes a sound of jingles and merriment. I have never been without them since the day I got married. *Again, part of our wedding ritual, bangles to a married girl, used to be as sacred as the Bindi and the Sindoor or the gold band in the west.* In fact in Northern India there is a religious ceremony on the morning of the wedding, (as Indian weddings are generally in the evening, after sunset) when the bride's maternal uncles put sets of bangles on her wrists with their blessings. These are made in red, white and gold with a specific sacred design but can have different combinations. This set of bangles is called a **'Choora'.** On these, the female relatives and friends of the bride then tie on little jingles, generally in gold, sometimes in silver, called **"Kaleeras"**. The *kaleeras* are taken off the day after the wedding, but the sacred bangles are worn for at least a month, sometimes a whole year when they are replaced with the everyday ones which can be gold, silver or glass.

Traditionally it was accepted that as long as the bride was wearing her **'choora'** she was not supposed to do any housework as the term 'new bride' was still applicable!

In America a film has been made on Bindis, in which a young Asian girl, who was singled out in class as different by her mates, eventually wins approval, when her mother comes up with the idea of sending packs of Bindis with her daughter to distribute in the class. The children are fascinated. With a different coloured dot on the forehead of each child, white, brown or black, the idea of sameness emerges. The theme of racial harmony is developed with a simple idea of a Bindi. Children are mesmerised by it, this I have seen myself on every social occasion that I have attended, as I always come home without it. My Bindi is always left behind on some child's, sometimes even a friend's, forehead as they would have been unable to take their eyes off it the whole evening.

Various provinces in India have their own styles of bangles. Delhi and Mumbai have small delicate gold ones; Uttar Pradesh is famous for its glitzy glass bangles. But the best known ones are from Jaipur in Rajasthan where they make them with different coloured sealing wax and while it is still warm and in the moulding stage they fix on little shapes of glass and make the most appealing of designs. Be careful with them if you ever have them, because if you ever leave them in the sun or indeed in any hot place, they will melt and lose their shape.

In 1973, ten months after arriving in Northern Ireland, I went to the Home office to get a work permit to take up a job. I was questioned for a long time as to who I was, when did I come to N.I, how did I support myself and the twin sons, where did I get the money, and so on. An hour later I realized that the girls behind the counter were not convinced that I was married as I had no wedding band on my finger which, in my world in India was not a social requirement. But then they did not understand that I had on my Bindi, my Bangles and my Sindoor. I did eventually get my work permit then; I hope I have made my point now.

4 MURGH
(Chicken)

Naariyal Masaala Murgh
(Chicken with creamed Coconut)

Murgh Makhani
(Spicy grilled Chicken in Tomato butter sauce)

Shahi Murgh
(Chicken curry with Almonds, Raisins & Cream)

Murgh Narangi
(Chicken curry with Orange & Sweet Corn)

Hara Masaala Murgh
(Chicken with fresh Coriander, Mint &Chillies)

Section

The more expensive of the meats, chicken meat is always served as a delicacy in India. Firm strong and tasty, chicken is still the preferred dish, possibly because, they are not, as yet, mass produced as in the west, and therefore still retain their flavour. Since they are farm reared, the chicken meat can sometimes be tough which has brought small chickens with less weight, to the forefront, which are called 'broilers'. Possibly, not as tasty as the big chickens these are never-the-less far easier to cook.

The art of cooking chicken as of meat has been acquired from the Mughals and Kashmiri's who make the most interesting of dishes; from the wonderful Biryaanis to the simple curries and then to the dry Tandoori meats; onto the more exotic curries like the *Makhani Murgh, Murgh Massalam, Hara masaala Murgh or Murgh Korma.*

A couple of points to note in cooking chicken; **firstly;** *chicken is never cooked with its skin on,* a fact that I had to, years ago, teach my butcher as I always had to ask him to skin the chickens for me. Now, the larger supermarkets have started to keep pre-packed skinned portions so there must be a greater demand for it even in the western food. Apart from the health foods perspective, as skin is technically pure fat, this layer also does not allow marinades and spices to penetrate through to the flesh leaving it quite bland. Also it gets flabby and soft when boiled in curries so it is best to start with the skin off. **Secondly;** *most of our Indian dishes require*

small pieces of chicken; they are easier to cook in the curries and get a more even coating of spices. But remember that, like meat, chicken also, is never boned. The pieces are cut with the bone. A difference between the preferences of the east and west is that the west prefers the lighter meat of the breast portion, a fact which took me a long time to understand as in India the majority would prefer the darker meat of the legs and thighs. Needless to say, these are the first pieces to be taken when serving, as in India chickens are still sold as whole, since the concept of joints being sold separately has not yet been marketed to any success.-

Here in the west chickens are economical to buy and convenient to cook as they are fleshy and tender and can be bought whole, quartered, or jointed. Only drumsticks can be bought if so desired or only wings. But what I can tell you is that I have found that the most flavoured dishes are the ones that have been cooked with the whole chicken, cut into pieces, instead of using only legs or only breast portions, which can only mean that different portions must have different flavours to contribute to the whole dish.

A final point to note is that organic or farm reared chicken is definitely a better product for the Indian dishes as they have a stronger flavour which absorb the spices better; they also retain their juices better when frying or roasting them in the Indian spices.

NAARIYAL MASAALA MURGH

(Chicken with creamed Coconut);

A variation South Indian dish particularly of the Kerala region, the Naariyal Masaala Murg has a sweet aromatic flavour. Very spicy in its original form, I have tempered it down, leaving it with **a hint of the sweetness of the coconut with the bite of a green chilli, accompanied by a typical flavour of South India in their curry leaves.** This is a good party dish and personally a great favourite of mine.

Recipe; Serves 4-5

Ingredients; Method

1 medium sized chicken, skinned, and cut into portions with the bone

12 -14 peppercorns, whole or partially crushed

6-8 curry leaves

1 teaspoon of black mustard seeds (optional)

1 medium sized onion, finely chopped

1 inch cube of ginger, finely chopped

6 cloves of garlic, finely chopped

1-2 green chillies, finely chopped

5-6 sprigs of fresh coriander, chopped

2 teaspoons of ground coriander seeds

1 teaspoon of ground cumin seeds

1 teaspoon of ground fenugreek seeds

1/2 teaspoon of paprika

1/2 teaspoon of red chillies (optional)

1 teaspoon of garam masala

1/4 of the slab of creamed coconut or 1 can of coconut milk

1 1/2 glasses of water or chicken stock

1/2 teaspoon of salt

4 tablespoons of oil

Butter for frying the chicken

For garnishing;

4 sprigs of fresh coriander, finely chopped, 1 teaspoon of fresh double cream, fresh curry leaves (optional)

(1) Heat the butter and 2 tablespoons of oil in a broad, heavy based pan. Add the chicken portions and fry them for 2-3 mins, to seal the juices in and make them golden brown. Set them aside.

(2) Soak the creamed coconut in half a glass of water and set it aside to let it dissolve while the masaala is being made.

(3) Now heat the rest of the oil in the pan. Add the peppercorns, mustard seeds and the curry leaves and fry for 1 min.

(4) Add the chopped onion. ginger, garlic, green chilli and fresh coriander and fry for 2-3 min or until golden brown.

(5) Put in the chicken pieces and fry again for 8-10 mins, or until the liquid, if there is any, is totally dried up.

(6) Add the liquid with the soaked coconut and add the rest of the water. Bring to the boil, lower the heat and stirring occasionally, let it simmer for 30-35 mins or until the chicken is cooked. Switch off the heat and let it sit for about 10 mins to finish off cooking. Check for the thickness of the gravy, taste the salt, garnish and serve hot.

Garnish;

With chopped fresh coriander, 1 teaspoon of double cream in the corner of the dish and, if using the fresh curry leaves, set them in the centre of the dish.

Serve;

Traditionally served with plain boiled rice, a yoghurt and a plain salad of onions and lime; But it also goes well with tandoori roti, a plain yoghurt and a green salad.

Overall cooking time:- 1 hour 10 mins

Mom's Tips

(1) For the sake of convenience chicken pieces, without the bone can be used but the flavour is distinctly better with the bone in the dish. Also organic or free range chicken has a distinctly better taste and substance to it.

(2) *If you are conscious of not using too much oil then omit step(1); do not fry the chicken and put it in raw in step (5).* You will then have to fry it for longer as there will be more liquid to dry up, but then you need to increase the cooking time by 10 mins.

(3) If, when checking the gravy before serving, you feel it is too thick, add a few tablespoons of boiling water and loosen up the curry; if it is too thin then boil it away but remember to stir it constantly, so that it does not stick to the bottom.

(4) **A good dish for freezing.** Make small packs, defrost as many as required. Reheat in the microwave.

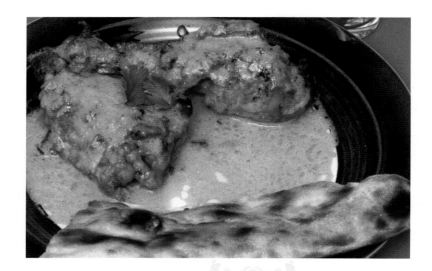

MURGH MAKHANI

(Spicy grilled Chicken in a Tomato butter sauce)

A dish of the north west of India, particularly the Panjab and Delhi; this is a dish of my childhood memories, the one that we would have nearly always when eating out. Probably this was due to the fact that tandoori chicken was impossible to make at home as it required a tandoor or a grill, so it was always an inaccessible dish; it was a long process to cook the chicken separately and the sauce separately; the ingredients were too rich and exotic. *An easy dish to make but difficult to acquire the right consistency,* a process which has been made easier now with the liquidizers and food processors. But the end result is always one that leaves you wanting to make this dish again and again. **The popular** *'Tikka Masaala'* **made popular by the supermarkets is a variation of this, but if you have this original traditional dish you may never want the commercial variety again.**

Recipe; Serves 4-6 people

Ingredients

1 med sized chicken skinned, cut into 8 pieces

For the marinade;

1 inch cube ginger finely chopped
4-5 cloves of garlic finely chopped
1 small green chilli finely chopped, optional
1 tablespoon fresh chopped coriander
2 tablespoons natural yoghurt
1 tablespoon oil
1 tablespoon lemon juice
1 teaspoon tandoori masaala
1/2 teaspoon garam masaala
1/2 teaspoon salt

For the sauce;

3 tablespoons of melted butter or ghee
1 inch cube of ginger chopped
3-4 cloves garlic chopped
1 green chilli chopped
1 tablespoon fresh chopped coriander
1/2 teaspoon red chilli, optional
1/2 teaspoon garam masaala
1 teaspoon roasted ground coriander
1 teaspoon roasted round cumin
1 teaspoon salt
1 big can of chopped tomatoes or 4 large tomatoes skinned, chopped
1/2 teaspoon sugar
1 teaspoon lemon juice
1 glass water
3 tablespoon of double cream

For garnishing;

teaspoon of cream, chopped coriander (optional), 2 green chilli

Method

(1) Prepare the marinade by mixing all the marinade ingredients together well; Ginger, garlic, chilli, coriander, yoghurt, oil, lemon juice, tandoori masaala, garam masaala and salt. Coat the chicken pieces with it; cover and leave the chicken for 4-5 hours.

(2) Preheat the oven to high. Put the chicken pieces in a baking dish and cook them for 35-40 mins or until they are cooked; turn them over once. Take them out of the oven and set them aside while you make the sauce.

(3) Heat the butter or ghee in a saucepan or a wok. Add the ginger, garlic and chilli and fry for 1 min Add the fresh coriander, red chilli, garam masaala, ground coriander and ground cumin and salt. Add tomatoes, canned or fresh and fry for 3-4 mins

(4) Add the sugar, lemon juice and water; bring to the boil lower the heat and simmer for 12-15 mins, switch off the heat and let it sit for 5 min

(5) Put this mixture into the liquidizer and whiz for 1-2 min till you have a smooth sauce. Pour it back into the wok and reheat or 2-3 min. Add the cream and let it heat through. Take it off the heat just before it comes to the boil.

(6) Arrange the chicken pieces in a serving dish. Pour the sauce over it and leave it sitting for 10-12 mins before serving. Serve hot

Garnish;
Spoon the cream in the centre; sprinkle coriander; arrange green chillies

Serve;
best with 'kale maan', tandoori roti and an onion salad, rice, a green salad and garlic bread; with any Indian meal.

Overall cooking time:-
10 mins to marinade; 1hr 15mins to cook

Mom's Tips

(1) **If there are extra juices left in the bottom of the pan after grilling the chicken put them in the tomato mixture for extra flavour.** If possible use organic or free range chicken as the taste of the dish is much better.

(2) *Better to make the dish the night before* as the dish will taste better when the flavours have permeated the chicken; reheat in the microwave or the oven otherwise the cream might split if heated on top of the cooker. If cutting down on the fat, use whipping cream instead of double cream.

(3) **You can freeze the dish; but it is better to freeze at step two** when the chicken is made. Make the sauce fresh and pour over the defrosted chicken.

SHAHI MURGH

(Chicken curry with Almonds, Raisins & Cream);

A Mughlai dish of the north-west region; a product of the Afghan cuisine; this, by *its very name denoted a dish that was rich and exotic, and was in fact 'fit for Royalty' which perhaps is the reason why this dish is made with boneless meat. This is unusual for Indian cuisine.* This is a lovely mild dish but one of the few that is finished off with rich ingredients; raisons, cashew nuts, almonds and cream, good for entertaining. It can be made the night before as the taste of the dish improves when time is given for the flavours to permeate through the chicken pieces.

Recipe; Serves -6

Ingredients

5-6 chicken breasts, boned and skinned

3 small green split cardamoms

3 cloves

1 inch piece of cinnamon, crushed

4-5 bay leaves, crushed

1 medium sized onion, peeled

1 inch cube of ginger, peeled

4-5 cloves of garlic, peeled

1 small green chilli

4 sprigs of fresh chopped coriander

1 small tomato chopped

1 teaspoon of ground coriander seed

1 teaspoon of ground roasted cumin seed

1/2 teaspoon of red chillies (optional)

1/2 teaspoon of paprika

1/2 teaspoon of garam masaala

1/2 teaspoon of turmeric

1 teaspoon of salt

2 tablespoons of yoghurt

20-25 kishmish (raisin)

8-10 **cashew nuts**, halved

6-8 **almonds** chopped

2-3 tablespoons of double cream

2 glasses of water

5-6 tablespoons of oil

For garnishing;

5-7 sprigs of fresh coriander, chopped;

2-3 fresh bay leaves (optional)

Method

(1) **First prepare the chicken.** Spread the breast pieces flat on a chopping board and cut it into strips, about an inch wide; 5-6 pieces per chicken breast. Lightly fry these in 2 tablespoons of oil and set them aside.

(2) **Now prepare the onion masaala.** Put the onion, ginger, garlic, chilli and fresh coriander in a food processor and process them together; alternatively, chop each of the ingredients very finely, mix them and set them aside.

(3) Heat the remaining oil on a medium heat in a karaahi or a broad based pan. Put in the cardamoms, cloves, cinnamon and bay leaves and fry for 30 secs.

(4) Add the onion masaala and fry until golden brown. This should take about 6-7 mins Then add the chopped tomato and fry for 1 min. Put in the dry masaala, coriander, cumin, red chillies, paprika, garam masaala, turmeric and salt and fry for 1 min.

(5) **Now add the yoghurt**, but slowly, bit by bit; add one teaspoon at a time, fry that and let it be absorbed before adding the next spoon. Finish all the yoghurt. Then add the chicken pieces, fry them in the masaala for 4-6 mins; add the water, mix well, bring to the boil, reduce the heat, cover the pan and simmer for 10 mins. Now add the raisins, cashew nuts, chopped almonds and simmer for another 7-10 mins. Add the double cream, mix well, cover the pan and switch off the heat. Let it sit for 5-7 mins to finish off cooking; then taste the salt, garnish and serve hot.

Garnish;

With chopped coriander and decorate with the fresh bay leaves

Serve;

With naan or tandoori roti, a dry vegetable and a yoghurt dish; or with a pulao rice and a green salad.

Overall cooking time; 1 hour

Mom's Tips

(1) *You can use boned and skinned thigh fillets if you prefer them* instead of the breast pieces. Remember to simmer the dish at stage (5) for 3-4 mins more as the thigh meat will take a bit longer to cook. Remember to make the dish with organic or free range chicken to get a better substance and taste to the dish.

(2) Always add the yoghurt little by little otherwise it gives out too much water which takes too long to dry and the flavour of the dish tends to be lost in that process.

(3) A good dish for freezing. Make small batches and defrost as many as required at a time. Reheat in the microwave.

MURGH NARANGI

(Chicken curry with Orange & Sweet corn)

A variation of a chicken curry this dish has proved a successful presentation in the western world as it has a **_tinge of_ _zingy sweetness_ _of the_ _orange_ _which offsets the spices._** This dish was made for the first time by chance. I had to go to India to see my father, leaving my twin teenage sons to be looked after and fed by their extremely busy father. Having arrived home late one night he tried to make a dish to satisfy the pallets of both; within reason; as it had to be within the norms of what was available in the house. One wanted chicken, the other loved sweet corn, there was an orange that needed to be used up, and he himself wanted a curry. **The compromise was so successful** that it was to be repeated often in the years to come for the family and more often that not, for entertaining.

Recipe; Serves 4-5 people

Ingredients

1 medium sized chicken skinned and cut into 10 pieces (or 5 legs skinned and cut into 10 pieces)

1 large onion, sliced or roughly chopped

1 inch cube of ginger thinly

6-7 cloves of garlic finely sliced

I small green chilli, finely chopped

2 large tomatoes chopped

8-10 peppercorns whole or crushed

2-3 bay leaves

1 teaspoon of ground coriander seeds

1 teaspoon of ground cumin seed seeds

1/2 teaspoon of turmeric

1/2 teaspoon of red chillies

1/2 teaspoon of garam masaala

1 teaspoon of salt

Juice of 1 med sized orange

1 small can of sweet corn or 1 cup of fresh corn

1-2 glasses of water

2-3 tablespoons of oil

For garnishing;
chopped coriander, wedges or slices of orange

Method

(1) Heat the oil and fry the peppercorns for 1-2 mins.

(2) Add the sliced onions, ginger, garlic and fry until golden brown. Add the tomatoes and fry till the oil begins to show in the pan.

(3) Add the dry spices; coriander, cumin, turmeric, red chillies, garam masaala, salt and fry for 1-2 min

(4) Add the chicken pieces and fry them in the masaala on a medium heat for 15-20 mins or until the juices dry up and the oil shows in the pan.

(5) Add the orange juice and the sweet corn and fry for 3-5 mins

(6) Add 1-2 glasses of water depending on how much gravy you would like in the dish, Cook for another 20 - 25 mins on low to med heat, or until the chicken is tender. Arrange the pieces in a shallow dish pour gravy over it and garnish. Serve hot.

Garnish;
Sprinkle coriander and arrange wedges of orange on the side.

Serve;
with rice, naan or garlic bread and a green salad; with any Indian meal or buffet

Overall cooking time:- 1hr to 1hr 10 mins

Mom's Tips

(1) **Be careful of the peppercorn;** if used whole they can be hard to bite and are very spicy when bitten.

(2) *Do not exceed 50 mins to 1hr from the time the chicken is added to the pan* as it is easy to overcook and then will fall off the bone when reheated to serve. It is also better to use free range chickens or organic chicken as they have more substance, less water and taste's better.

(3) **A good dish to freeze.** It can be reheated on the hob then arranged and garnished.

HARA MASAALA MURGH

(Chicken with fresh Coriander, Mint & Chillies);

A flavour from North India, this dish is more particularly from the Delhi region. More modern than traditional, this dish has its origin in the party hostesses trying out new dishes in an effort to create versatility. I had it for the first time in a family friend's house in America, and since then I have made it with slight variation here in Britain with great success. *It is mild in spices with a base of fresh herbs, mainly coriander, with a touch of mint and a few green chillies,* which gives it the unusual and delightful aroma of its own, and its name which translated simply means the chicken dish with a green masaala

Recipe; Serves 4-5

Ingredients

1 medium sized chicken, skinned and cut into 10-12 portions with the bones

2 black cardamoms split

5-6 cloves

1 stick of cinnamon, 1 1/2 inches long

10-12 peppercorns, whole or crushed

1 small onion, finely chopped

1/2 inch cube of ginger

6 cloves of garlic

2 teaspoons of ground coriander seeds

1/2 teaspoon of paprika

1/2 teaspoon of red chillies

1 teaspoon of garam masaala

1/2 teaspoon of turmeric

2 teaspoons of salt

3 tablespoons of natural yoghurt

1 large bunch of fresh coriander, 100 gm; washed and finely chopped

5-6 sprigs of mint, washed, finely

1-3 green chillies, finely chopped

Butter or oil for frying the chicken

1 1/2 glasses of water or stock

3-4 tablespoons of oil

For garnishing;

1 teaspoon of fresh double cream(optional), 2-3 fresh red chillies or a slice of tomato

Method

(1) Heat the butter and 2 tablespoons of oil on a high heat in a karaahi or a broad heavy based pan. Fry the chicken portions, 2-3 mins on each side to seal the juices in. They should be golden brown. Set them aside.

(2) Heat the rest of the oil in the same pan. Add the cardamoms, cloves, cinnamon and black peppercorns and fry for 1-2 mins.

(3) Add the chopped onion, ginger, garlic, chilli and fry for 3-4 mins or until they are golden brown.

(4) Add the spices, coriander, paprika, red chillies, turmeric and fry for 1 mins.

(5) Put in the yoghurt, a spoon at a time, stirring constantly and frying the mixture till the liquid has evaporated of each spoonful before adding the next.

(6) Start adding the chopped herb mixture of coriander and mint, a spoonful at a time and frying off the liquid of each spoonful before adding the next, till all the mixture is finished. Keep frying for another 4-5 mins.

(7) Add the chicken pieces, fry for another 10-12 mins.

(8) Add one to one and a half glass of water, or stock, close the lid and let it simmer for 30-35 mins, stirring it occasionally. Switch off the heat and let it sit for 10-15 mins to finish odd cooking in the steam. Then check the thickness of the herb gravy, taste the salt, garnish and serve hot.

Garnish;

Put a spoon of fresh double cream (optional), 2-3 small fresh red chillies or a slice of tomato on the side

Serve;

Best with a tandoori roti or chapaati, yoghurt, and a tomato and onion salad; or as an accompaniment to any daal or dry vegetable.

Overall cooking time:- 1 hour 15 mins.

Mom's Tips

(1) Boned pieces of chicken can be used for this dish if you want, but the flavour is better if the pieces have the bone with them. Again the taste of organic or free range chicken is far better in these dishes.

(2) Everything needs to be very finely chopped for this dish, if you have a food processor then chop the onion, ginger, chilli and garlic together in it; then process the coriander and mint together.

(3) Make sure to fry the yoghurt and the herb mixture bit by bit or the liquid will not dry up properly.

(4) If, at the end you feel you want more curry in the dish, add a couple of tablespoons of boiling water; or if you want it drier, them boil it rapidly for 2-3 mins, stirring constantly.

(5) A good dish for freezing. Make small packs, and when required defrost as many as required. Reheat in the microwave.

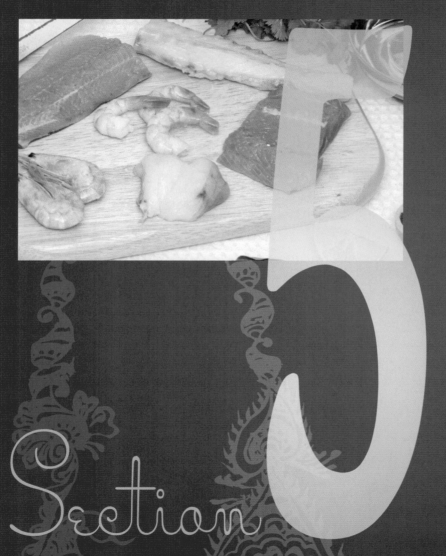

MACHHI AUR JHINGA

(Fish and Prawns);

Rai Vali Machhi
(Fish curry with Mustard)

Talli Machhi
(Spicy fried Fish)

Naariyal Vali Machhi
(Fish in Coconut curry)

Jhinga Masaala
(Dry spicy Prawns)

Machhi Rasadaar
(Fish in a spicy Tomato curry)

Section 5

Northern India is bordered by the vast Himalayan range of mountains which are well known, but even longer than that, but probably much less known, is the sea coastline of India which borders the East and the whole of the south, coming up to Bombay in the west. So it goes without saying that **the sea fish, prawns, lobsters and crabs are in abundance in these areas.** Each province has its own spices and traditional culinary methods to give the seafood its own distinctive taste; Bengal works mostly with a mustard base, Madras and Kerala have a lot of coconut so they are popular for their coconut paste, Goa is popular for its prawns, grilled and curried, Bombay, being cosmopolitan, is famous for its crabs and lobsters. *Fish is generally served with rice,* again, possibly due to geographical topography whereby Bengal and the South are rice growing areas. In Bengal the first solids that a baby is given at the age of three months, is pureed rice and fish.

Whereby the fish is generally curried in the south, it is fried or barbecued in the north and then, keeping in tune with the cuisine of the north it is accompanied by tandoori rotis or exotic rice dishes. Generally, as in the south, the flavour of fish or prawns is best enjoyed with plain boiled rice.

However the north has much less fish, which when available, is essentially river fish, and in my childhood, to have a fish meal was exciting and adventurous. Either it was a celebration of some sort or somebody went out and caught the fish at the stream. The names of those fish would be quite

unfamiliar here, like Malli, Singhaara, or Pomfret, but they have a firm flesh and do not fall apart when making curries or barbecuing, as we do not always use flour or crumbs or a batter to hold it. Here, I have tried to find comparatives and have come up with Monkfish tails, or Hake which are firm fish, but Trout and Salmon are also tasty and can be worked with, as long as the skin is kept on while cooking and then discarded if so desired. Plaice is an excellent stand-in for the Pomfret and is ideal for some of our fried fish varieties although the Pomfret has more flesh on it.

Although frozen fish is abundantly available in all the supermarkets, there is nothing quite like fresh fish. Even better is the fish that has been caught in the morning and set on the dining table the same night. For the prawn dishes try and get large king sized ones if possible. **It is quite traditional to rub salt, pepper and lemon juice on the fish and leave it covered for three to four hours before starting to make any dish.** This reduces the fishy smell. Also remember that fish is a soft and bland food and consequently will require less of spices than meat, chicken, and even some vegetables.

A final point to note; in India dish is treated as a non vegetarian food and as such the rules of vegetarian food will apply to this as well; keep the fish products well away from the vegetarian food while cooking; do not add fish stock to the vegetable dishes. I have heard it being said here in the west; 'I am a vegetarian',' I only eat fish'. Eating only white meat is not the same thing as being a vegetarian.

RAI VALI MACHHI

(Fish curry with Mustard);

This is a typically Bengali dish and a favourite of the eastern region. Originally made with small oily fish with a lot of bones, which give the dish taste of its own, I have tried to give a similar flavour by using herrings, sometimes even mackerel. A lightly *spiced dish*, as I have toned down the chilli content, this is a delightful variation for those who like fish and the taste of mustard. I have used the commercial mustard powder, but in India where this was not available the mustard seeds were finely ground to make the paste, hence the name.

Recipe; Serves 4

Ingredients

8 herring fillets, boned, or 1/2 kg of mackerel or trout

2 teaspoons of mustard seeds

8 kari patta

3 green chillies, deseeded, cut lengthways

1 small green pepper, diced

1 small red pepper diced

1 small yellow pepper, diced

2 glasses of water

3 tablespoons of oil

Paste;

2 teaspoons of mustard powder

1 teaspoon of turmeric

1/2 teaspoon of paprika

1/2 teaspoon of red chillies

1 teaspoon of salt

For garnishing; fresh chopped coriander or and a pinch of garam masaala

Method

(1) **First make the paste** in half a cup of water with the mustard powder, turmeric, paprika, red chillies and salt. Set aside.

(2) Heat the oil in a heavy based pan. Fry the mustard seeds for 1 min or till the popping sound starts. Add the kari patta and the green chillies and fry for 1/2 min

(3) Put in the spicy paste water and add another one and a half glasses of water. Bring it to the boil and simmer for 5 mins

(4) Drop in the herring fillets and bring to boil again. Then reduce the heat, cover the pan and let it simmer for 5 mins

(5) Add the diced peppers. Again cover the pan and let it simmer for another 10 mins. Switch off the heat and leave it sitting for 10 mins to finish off cooking. Check the gravy; it will be thin gravy; taste the salt, garnish and serve hot.

Garnish;
With chopped coriander.

Serve;
With boiled rice, spicy cabbage, and an onion and tomato salad.

Overall cooking time:- 35 mins.

Mom's Tips

(1) *Fresh herrings taste the best,* but if you are unable to get them use smoked herring; or even fresh or smoked mackerel.

(2) It is not a good fish for freezing, as the fish does not retain the same flavour.

TALLI MACHHI

(Spicy fried Fish);

A north Indian dish, this a great favourite of my family. *It can be made with any fish;* monkfish tails and hake is particularly good, but steaks or even fillets of a trout or a small salmon are tasty and hold together well, as long as the skin is left on. **A popular winter snack,** in Chandigarh, in the Punjab in India, this fish is fried in front of you, and sold by the roadside vendors in disposable banana leaf plates with mint chutney on the side. It can be served with cocktails before dinner; as a starter; or as an additional dish at a party table.

Recipe; Serves 3-4

Ingredients

1 medium sized trout, washed and cleaned or 1/2 kg of filleted fish with its skin

Oil for frying

Marinade;

1 inch cube of ginger, roughly chopped

3 cloves of garlic,

1 green chilli

1 tablespoon of chopped fresh coriander

1/2 teaspoon of ground coriander seeds

1/2 teaspoon of ground cumin seeds

1/2 teaspoon of paprika

1 teaspoon of garam masaala

Pinch of turmeric

1/2 teaspoon of salt

1 tablespoon of lemon juice

1 tablespoon of cold cooking oil

Paste;

1 tablespoon of gram flour

1/2 tablespoon of plain flour

1 tablespoon of water

For garnishing;

rings of raw onion, lemon wedges

Method

(1) First prepare the fish. Cut the head and discard it. Cut the rest into steaks, about 3/4 inches thick. There should be about 6-7 steaks. Alternatively the fish can be filleted and then cut into pieces, as large or as small as required. **Keep the skin on the pieces as it will hold it together when cooking.** Set it aside.

(2) Make the marinade. Put the ginger, garlic and chilli in a mortar and pestle and grind them into a paste. Then add the dry spices, coriander, cumin, paprika, garam masaala, turmeric and salt followed by the lemon juice and the cooking oil; mix well.

(3) Coat the fish pieces well with the marinade, making sure that each piece is covered with it; cover and set aside for 2-3 hours.

(4) Make a paste with the gram flour, plain flour and the water and mix it well with the fish. Now you are ready to shallow fry it.

(5) Heat the oil in a non stick wok or a heavy broad based frying pan. There should be less than one inch of oil in the pan and no more. Put the fish pieces in gently, one at a time, about 3-4 in a batch; fry for about 3-4 mins each side or until golden brown. Drain on kitchen paper and keep warm while the second batch is done also. Arrange on a flat dish, garnish and serve.

Garnish;

With raw onion rings and lemon wedges.

Serve;

With a mint or coriander chutney as a starter; it can also be served as a main course with the chutney, coleslaw, a green salad and a jacket potato or potato chips or with any Indian meal.

Overall cooking time:- 20 mins preparation time and 20 mins to cook .

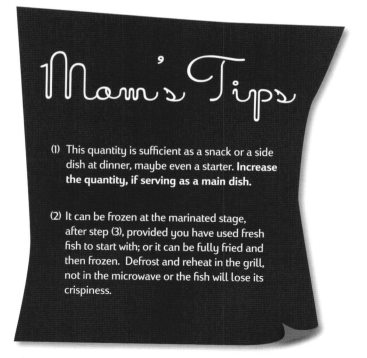

Mom's Tips

(1) This quantity is sufficient as a snack or a side dish at dinner, maybe even a starter. **Increase the quantity, if serving as a main dish.**

(2) It can be frozen at the marinated stage, after step (3), provided you have used fresh fish to start with; or it can be fully fried and then frozen. Defrost and reheat in the grill, not in the microwave or the fish will lose its crispiness.

NAARIYAL VALI MACHHI

(Fish in Coconut curry):

A variation of an extremely delightful south Indian dish from Kerala called the **'Fish Molee'.** It is possibly one of the nicest curried fish dishes in the Indian cuisine; a great favourite of mine. Traditionally a very hot dish it can be made as mild as one wants to by regulating the red chillies, or even substituting them totally by paprika. De-seeding the green chillies would retain their flavour, while reducing their pungent properties. *It tastes best if made with a firm fish,* like monkfish tails or hake as the pieces do not disintegrate or flake while cooking or lifting out of the dish to arrange on a serving plate.

Recipe; Serves 4-5

Ingredients

1/2 kg of Monkfish tails, cut into 1 1/2 inch pieces or any other fish

Marinade for the fish,

2 tablespoon of lemon juice

1/2 teaspoon of salt

1/2 teaspoon of garam masaala

Curry,

10 leaves of kari patta (leaves).

1 teaspoon of black mustard seeds (optional)

1 medium sized onion, peeled

1 inch cube of ginger, peeled

4-5 cloves of garlic, peeled

2 -3 small green chillies, deseeded

4 sprigs of fresh coriander, washed

1/4 of the slab of creamed coconut

1 teaspoon of ground coriander seeds

1 teaspoon of ground fenugreek seeds

1/2 teaspoon of garam masaala

1/2 teaspoon of red chillies

1/2 teaspoon of paprika

1/2 teaspoon of turmeric

1/2 teaspoon of salt

1 1/2 glasses of water

2-3 tablespoons of oil

For garnishing;

5-6 sprigs of fresh coriander, chopped, 3-4 small green or red chillies, and pinch of garam masaala

Method

(1) First prepare the fish. Wash well, pat the pieces dry and rub the salt, garam masaala and lemon juice and set aside

(2) Now prepare the masaala. Put the onion, ginger, garlic, green chillies and fresh coriander in a food processor and process them or chop them very finely.

(3) Put the creamed coconut in 1 glass of hot water, mix it and set it aside.

(4) Heat the oil on a medium heat in a heavy based pan. Fry the onion masaala with kari patta and black mustard seeds until the onion is golden brown. Then add the dry ingredients, coriander, fenugreek, paprika, red chillies, garam masaala, turmeric and salt and fry for 1 min.

(5) Put in the water with the soaked creamed coconut, mix well and gently bring it to boil on a low heat and simmer for 5 mins. Add the fish and the rest of the water gently mix it and bring it to the boil. Still on low heat simmer it for about 15 mins or until the fish is cooked. Mix gently; check the thickness of the curry; taste the salt, garnish and serve the fish hot.

Garnish;

Sprinkle the chopped coriander, arrange the green leaves in the centre of the dish and finish with sprinkling garam masaala.

Serve;

With boiled rice, a green salad and a chilli and mango pickle; add a side dish of any dry spiced vegetable

Overall cooking time:- 50 mins to 1 hour.

Mom's Tips

(1) The fish should be a firm fish like monkfish tails or hake as there is less likelihood of it disintegrating when cooking it. However, I have cooked this dish with salmon steaks and trout fillets by leaving the skin on the pieces as that then reduces the chances of the pieces breaking up. For the same reason once the dish is cooked arrange it in the serving dish and leave it aside to reheat in the microwave

(2) Do not use the commercial coconut milk instead of the creamed coconut as there is a difference in the taste and flavour even though the soaked creamed coconut does become coconut milk.

(3) **If you do not like the smell of fish you can fry the pieces of fish and set them aside before you start making the dish.** I try and avoid the frying to use less oil; however I like the flavour of fish and anyway the rubbing of salt, garam masaala and lemon juice does reduce the fishy smell.

(4) *A good dish for freezing.* Once defrosted, reheat in the microwave.

JHINGA MASAALA

(Dry Spicy Prawns)

A dish equally popular in Bengal and the southern regions of India as both are coastal areas. Having lived in the landlocked province of Punjab in the north for the first thirty years of my life I had never had much fish and never prawns Then I went to Mumbai and was introduced to a variety of seafood ; I was hooked on prawns, small ones, large ones, uncooked ones, with or without shells, tiger prawns; all varieties of them. I learnt to cook them, experimented with them as *prawns are mild to the extent of being bland and cannot take much spice or they will lose their individual flavour.* This is one of my favourite ways of spicing them as this way they can be served with drinks as a snack. Put a few cocktail sticks in the dish and the prawns can be lifted with wrapping the masaala round them like a thick dip.

Recipe; 4-5 people

Ingredients

20-25 Tiger prawns (or as many per person as required)

Marinade

Juice of half a lemon

1 teaspoon garam masaala

1/2 teaspoon of salt

Curry

1 large onion; half chopped; half sliced

1inch cube of ginger thinly sliced

8-10 cloves of garlic thinly sliced

1 green chilli thinly sliced

2 tomatoes chopped

1/2 green or 1/2 red pepper chopped (optional)

1 tablespoon of chopped fresh coriander

1 teaspoon of ground coriander seeds

1/2 teaspoon of red chillies

1/2 teaspoon of garam masaala

1/2 teaspoon of salt

2-3 tablespoons of oil

For garnishing;

Chopped coriander, 5-7 thin slices of green and red peppers, wedges of lemon

Method

(1) Wash and prepare the prawns by removing the skin if on. Put in a bowl with the lemon juice, garam masaala and salt and leave to marinade for an hour

(2) Heat the oil in a frying pan. Fry the onion, garlic, cloves and chilli and fry until golden brown. Add the tomatoes and the green peppers and the chopped coriander and fry for 2-3 mins.

(3) Add the spices; ground coriander, red chillies garam masaala and salt. Fry for 1-2 mins.

(4) Add the prepared prawns; mix in well with the masaala in the pan; cover; lower the heat and let the flavours mix for 3-4 mins. Take off the heat. Arrange in a shallow dish, garnish; serve hot

Garnish;

sprinkle the chopped coriander and arrange the wedges on the side of the plate

Serve;

As a starter; with boiled rice and an onion salad; as a side dish to any Indian meal

Overall Cooking time:- 20 to 25 mins.

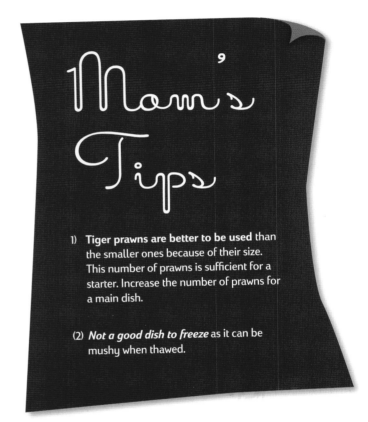

Mom's Tips

1) **Tiger prawns are better to be used** than the smaller ones because of their size. This number of prawns is sufficient for a starter. Increase the number of prawns for a main dish.

(2) *Not a good dish to freeze* as it can be mushy when thawed.

MACHHI RASADAAR

(Fish in a spicy Tomato curry);

Fish is a basic food item of the coastal regions all over the world basically because of its availability from the water; the same is true of the coast line of the south of India and even more so of the province of Bengal which sits on the Bay of Bengal in the east. I am from Punjab which has mughlai influence on its cuisine which is based on meat and chicken but I was always very fond of fish which would make my mother call me a 'bengaalan'. So I experimented with fish and made this *curry with a Panjabi style with a thick sauce* which was more appealing to the family.

Recipe; Serves 4-5 people

Ingredients

Salmon fillet cut into 2 inch cubes; (8cubes) or1/2 kg of any fish

Marinade;

1/4 teaspoon of salt

1/2 teaspoon of garam masaala

1 tablespoon of lemon juice

Curry;

1 onion finely chopped

1 teaspoon of whole black mustard seed (optional)

8 leaves of Kari patta

1 inch cube of ginger finely chopped

6-7 cloves of garlic finely chopped

1 green chilli finely chopped

1 tablespoon of fresh coriander chopped

1 small can of chopped tomatoes 250 gms or 3 tomatoes skinned and chopped

1 teaspoon of ground coriander seeds

1 teaspoon of ground cumin seeds

1 teaspoon of ground fenugreek seeds

1/2 teaspoon of turmeric

1/2 teaspoon of red chilli or paprika

1 teaspoon of salt

1 1/2 glasses of water

2-3 tablespoons of oil

For garnishing;

chopped coriander; 2 green chilli; garam masaala

Method

(1) Rub the salt and the garam masaala in the fish pieces and sprinkle the lemon juice. Set aside.

(2) Heat the oil in a wok or a saucepan. Add the mustard seeds and the curry leaves and fry for 30 secs or until sizzling. Add the onion, ginger, garlic and chilli and fry until golden brown. Add the tomatoes and the chopped coriander and fry for 1 mt.

(3) Add the ground spices; coriander, cumin, fenugreek, turmeric, chilli and salt and fry for 1 min or until the oil shows in the pan.

(4) Add 1 1/2 glasses of water and bring to the boil. Let it simmer for 5 mins so that the flavours blend.

(5) Add the fish pieces and let it simmer for 8-10 mins. Switch off the cooker and let it sit on the warm plate to keep warm. Serve hot.

Garnish;

sprinkle chopped coriander and garam masaala; arrange the green chillies on the side.

Serve;

serve with boiled rice and a tomato and onion salad.

Overall cooking time:- 35-40 mins

Mom's Tips

(1) **Don't overcook the fish** as it will fall apart when serving; for the same reason don't stir it more than once; **Salmon or monkfish** is better as they are firm fish; **If salmon leave the skin on while cooking** to hold the pieces together. It can be taken off while eating or before serving.

(2) It is a **good dish to freeze.**

DAALS

(Pulses and Lentils);

Channas
(Chickpea curry)

Malka Masar ki Daal
(Red Lentil curry)

Rajmaan
(Kidney Bean curry)

Sookhe Maan
(Dry spiced Lentils, Urad washed)

Kale Maan
(Black Lentil curry)

Section 6

Pulses, which broadly will include all the dried peas, beans and lentils, are as much part of the staple diet in India as rice or bread. **Cheap and economical,** yet high in protein value it is, on the one hand, sometimes the only accompaniment for the poor man's meal; on the other hand, a dinner table, set with Indian food, can never be considered complete without at least one dish of a daal on the menu. At this point the word daal is being used in a broad spectrum including all of the above, although strictly speaking, it denotes only lentils.

The versatility of these is enormous; perhaps because of the various groups of lentils and their further sub-sections. There are *five main groups*; *Urad, Moong, Masar, Arhar and Channe*; the first two of which come in three forms, whole split and washed, the rest in whole and split, each with its own flavour, texture and taste. These daals can be cooked on their own added to vegetables or meat dishes, or, some, like the *Urad washed* and the *Moong washed,* can be ground into a paste, beaten into a batter and made into delicious savoury snacks called **'Vadas',** eaten by themselves or made into a form of an exotic yoghurt dish. The same paste can be fried in oil and with the addition of sugar, almonds and kishmish made into a sweet called *'daal ka halva.' Chickpeas, Kidney beans and Black eyed beans* come in just the one form each, but again, the variations of dishes they can be used in is tremendous; from curries to salads; and then again being mixed and matched with vegetables and meats in different variations of provincial dishes.

The most popular daal in North Indian food is the whole Urad, or popularly known as **'Kale Maan',** a must for a party or for an Indian restaurant meal. The most well known of the daals here in the west is the Masar, commonly known as red split lentils; in its raw form it is pink in colour but yellow when it is

cooked. Here it is generally used for soups. In India it is cooked with spices and herbs, and is finished with a **'Tarka',** sometimes known as *'Bagaar'*, which is basically chopped onion, tomatoes, and spices fried in butter or ghee. Absolutely delicious. In Indian restaurants here in the west, Channe ki Daal with the garnish is known as 'Tarka Daal'. A note here to say that *Tarka goes on top of every Daal*; not necessarily with all the ingredients; it may be with just whole mustard seeds, or with only cumin seed, sometimes just hot butter.

By now you will have realized that Indian cooking is, to a large extent based on herbs and spices which have digestive properties, but some of these will react even better if cooking with particular vegetables or meat; e.g. cardamoms, cinnamon or cloves are very good for rice or meat dishes. In the case of daals, the addition of ginger garlic and turmeric makes them more digestible particularly the whole daals, the chickpeas and beans.

In my young days, lentils used to be made in a utensil called the **'Haandi',** sometimes also known as a **'Degchi'.** This had a small base, just big enough to sit on a stove, and then it ballooned out in the middle, and then narrowed down again to a similar size as the base. This shape retained the steam in the pan and 'speeded up the cooking'; an academic phrase as the whole lentils or the peas and beans took at least 3-4 hours to cook anyway. The Haandis were generally made of copper or brass, but there were clay Haandis in existence as well, although they could be set only on a slow fire, and took twice the time to cook, but the end result was out of this world. Because of the time and effort it took to cook these dishes, one of them was always part of our Sunday lunch in those bygone days. The pressure cookers today have speeded up the process; these dishes can now be made oftener; but

that taste and atmosphere is difficult to acquire.

A word here regarding the Pressure cookers; it is difficult to cook hard peas and beans without them. Since the makes vary, be careful to study the literature of the cooker before you attempt to cook with it. The cooking time may vary; experiment with it and with practice you will come to enjoy working with it.

CHANNAS

(Chickpea curry);

Chickpeas have become very popular in the west in the recent times as they have become part of the range of foods available in health food shops, and are generally used in dips and salads. *Part of the Indian food scene for centuries,* they are curried in this cooking and make an excellent dish as they are strong peas and absorb spices very well. Also called **'Chole'**, it is traditionally a dish from North India, and make a good combination with three types of Indian breads, *bhaturas, naans, and pooris* .If only boiled they can be added to tangy salads, or as Greeks do, ground into a paste and made into a dip. The Chickpea curry can be had as a main meal for vegetarians or as an accompaniment to savoury snacks like pakoras or samosas. They can be cooked dry spiced, or with gravy. They can be added to meat dishes or vegetables. If the above breads are not available they can be served with a rice dish or even plain bread or baps. **The versatility of these Chickpeas is enormous.** Here is the recipe for a basic Chickpea dish.

Recipe; Serves 4-6

Ingredients

2 glasses of chickpeas (channas) washed and soaked overnight

4-5 glasses of water

1 medium sized onion, finely chopped

1 inch cube of ginger, finely chopped

5-6 cloves of garlic, chopped or crushed

2 small tomatoes chopped,

1 green chilli, finely chopped

4 bay leaves

2 teaspoons of ground coriander seeds

1 teaspoon of ground cumin seeds

1 teaspoon of ground fenugreek seeds

1 teaspoon of paprika

1/2 teaspoon of red chillies (optional)

1 teaspoons of garam masaala

1/2 teaspoon of turmeric

1/2 teaspoons of salt

4-5 sprigs of fresh coriander, finely chopped

1 teaspoon of lemon juice

1/2 spoon of amchur (optional)

3 tablespoons of oil

For garnishing;

Knob of butter; 3-4 sprigs of fresh coriander or parsley, chopped, rings of raw onion, lemon wedges, small thin potato chips(optional)

Method

(1) Wash and drain the soaked chickpeas and set aside.

(2) Put the chickpeas in the pressure cooker with 4-5 glasses of water, 2 clove of garlic, half inch cube of ginger, 1 teaspoon of salt, a pinch of garam masaala and the bay leaves. Bring to the boil, put the weight on and give full pressure for 15 mins. Leave the cooker aside to cool, which could take up to half an hour, then take the weight off. Check that the chickpeas are cooked, drain the chickpeas and keep aside, but save the water in which the chickpeas were boiled.

(3) Heat the oil in a heavy based pan. Add the onion, garlic and ginger till golden brown. Add all the dry spices, coriander, cumin, fenugreek, paprika, red chillies, turmeric, garam masaala, and the rest of the salt. Fry for 1 min.

(4) Add the tomatoes, green chillies, and the fresh coriander and fry for 2-3 mins.

(5) Add the cooked and drained chickpeas and fry again for 4-5 mins.

(6) Add 2 glasses of the water in which the chickpeas were boiled; if there is less water left make up the rest by adding hot boiling water. Simmer for 25-30 mins. Add the lemon juice and amchur just before taking it off the heat; taste the salt, garnish and serve hot.

Garnish;

Put a knob of butter in the centre. Sprinkle chopped coriander or parsley. Can also decorate with sliced fried onions or rings of raw onion, thin potato chips and lemon wedges.

Serve;

With bhaturas, naans or pooris and a yoghurt; alternatively with rice, boiled or onion pulao, with a green salad.

Overall Cooking Time:- 1 hour.

Mom's Tips

(1) **Always soak Chickpeas for at least 4-6 hours preferably overnight, as they are hard peas and will not otherwise cook properly,** not even in a pressure cooker.

(2) If you do not have a pressure cooker or do not like to use one, use two tins of cooked chickpeas for this recipe and omit step (2). If you decide to use a pressure cooker, *remember to follow the directions of the cooker and do not open it till the steam inside has subsided.*

(3) Take a few chickpeas, mash them and put them back in the dish to give it a slightly thicker consistency, if you so desire. I tend to do that when I make this dish.

(4) In the old traditional method of cooking chickpeas were always cooked in an iron pot or iron **karaahi**, which made the dish dark in colour. To give a similar colour, if preferred, add a tea bag to the chickpeas before bringing it to the boil, in step (2). Discard it later.

(5) A very good dish for freezing. Individual portions are a good idea if small quantities are required at a time. Reheat in the microwave or on the hob.

MALKA MASAR KI DAAL

(Red Lentil curry)

A north Indian dish it is as popular as the Irish stew in Ireland. A firm favourite of my husband and mother- in-law, it is simple to make and easy to gather up ingredients for, as this particular lentil is **available in any corner shop or grocery store** and is part of the western cooking, particularly in its range of soups. A mild dish, it can be **part of the fat free diet** as the butter garnishing is generally added after the lentil is cooked.

Recipe; Serves 4-5

Ingredients

1 Glass of red lentils

1 medium tomato chopped

1 inch cube of ginger finely chopped

1 green chilli finely chopped

1/2 teaspoon of coriander

1/2 teaspoon of turmeric

1/2 teaspoon of red chillies or paprika

1 teaspoon of salt

3-4 glasses of water

Tarka;

A knob of butter,

1 small onion chop chopped,

1 teaspoon of whole cumin seed,

1/4 teaspoon of red chillies

For garnishing;

1 tablespoon of chopped coriander

Method

(1) Wash the lentils thoroughly. Put them in a sauce pan. Add the water and all the other ingredients; tomato, coriander, turmeric, chillies, salt.

(2) Bring to the boil, Reduce heat to medium, partially cover the pan and simmer for 1/2 hour or until the cooked lentils achieve the desired consistency. Stir regularly. Check the salt. Set aside.

(3) Make the tarka; heat the butter, fry the onions until golden brown, add the whole cumin seed for 1 min. Take it off the heat. Add the red chilli. Set aside.

Garnish;

Heat the daal and put in the serving dish. Heat the butter garnish and pour it on the daal. Sprinkle with chopped fresh coriander.

Serve;

With rice or chapaathis, accompanied by a dry spiced vegetable or meat dish, natural yoghurt, onion and tomato salad and mango pickle or chutney.

Overall cooking time:- 35 - 40 mins.

Mom's Tips

(1) Be careful when bringing the lentils to boil. **Reduce the heat immediately as it is quick to boil over;** never cover the saucepan fully or again it will boil over.

(2) *If you want it mild with only a hint of chilli and no more,* halve them and lift them out when the lentils are cooked.

(3) **Not a good dish for freezing** but it can be made 4-6 hours earlier and reheated in the microwave or on the hob.

RAJMAAN

(Kidney Bean curry);

Kidney Beans are small kidney shaped beans, generally dark maroon in colour, although there is a pale variety available in Indian shops which is stronger in taste. This is an excellent dish, **rich in protein,** and very popular in Northern India, particularly in the Panjab, and makes a good meal with rice which can be just boiled or made into a pulao. The combination of Rajmaan and rice is as popular in North India as fish and chips are in Britain. This combination is traditionally popular as a Tuesday afternoon lunch as that day is considered the holy day of the week by the Hindus and therefore a day without meat or fish, a vegetarian day

These are hard beans and need to be softened by a soaking process, although the pressure cooker now cooks them in a short span of time. Before the pressure cooker days kidney beans used to take a long time to cook, in fact the best I have had used to be in a small back-street restaurant in Delhi, where they used to be left cooking in a clay pot over a low coal fire for 7-8 hours and the end result was out of this world.

Recipe; Serves 4-6

Ingredients

2 glasses of kidney beans (washed and soaked overnight)

1 medium sized onion, grated, or finely chopped

1 inch cube ginger, grated or chopped

3-4 cloves of garlic, chopped or crushed

1 green chilli, finely chopped

2 tomatoes, chopped

1 teaspoon of ground coriander seeds

1 teaspoon of ground cumin seeds

1/2 teaspoon of red chillies (optional)

1/2 teaspoon of garam masaala

1/2 teaspoon of turmeric

1 teaspoons of salt

4-5 glasses of water

2 tablespoons of cooking oil

For garnishing;

5 sprigs of fresh coriander or parsley, finely chopped and a pinch of garam masaala

Method

(1) Wash and drain the kidney beans and set aside.

(2) Heat the oil in a pressure cooker. Add the onion, ginger and garlic and brown them.

(3) Add the ground coriander, ground cumin, red chillies, garam masaala and turmeric. Fry them for 1-2 mins.

(4) Add the tomatoes and green chilli and fry for 2 mins.

(5) Add the kidney beans and mix well.

(6) Add 4-5 glasses of water and bring to the boil. Put the weight on the cooker and give full pressure for 15 mins, leave to cool, which could take up to half an hour, and then take the weight off.

(7) Open the pan, mix well, and make sure that the beans have softened and then close the lid and simmer once again for 10 mins with the lid closed. Taste the salt; garnish and serve hot.

Garnish;

sprinkle with chopped coriander, if desired sprinkle with garam masaala.

Serve;

with boiled or pea pulao rice, green salad and raita; any dry vegetable can be served with it.

Overall Cooking Time:- 1 hour.

Mom's Tips

(1) Even when using a pressure cooker, **always soak the Kidney beans at least for 4-6 hours preferably overnight, or the beans will not soften.** Always drain the water in which the Kidney beans have been soaked.

(2) Take a few beans and mash them and put back in the gravy to give it a slightly thicker consistency if you so desire. I tend to do that when I make this dish.

(3) With practice, you will learn to cook according to your own pressure cooker and your own variety of beans as sometimes they may take a minute more or a minute less to soften.

(4) If you do not have a pressure cooker or have hesitation in using one, then omit the cooking of the beans Instead, add two tins of cooked Kidney beans at step 5, simmer for 20 mins, mash some beans for the consistency and serve. *If you do use a pressure cooker, be sure to follow the directions of the cooker, and do not attempt to open it till the steam inside has subsided.*

(5) An ideal dish for freezing. Do so in small quantities and reheat as required.

SOOKHE MAAN

(Dry spiced Lentils, Urad washed);

A firm favourite of the rural Panjab, this is a north Indian dish. An easy dish to make, it used to be slightly tricky as the daal is a soft product when cooked and to keep the grains fluffy and whole and yet have them cooked was not easy. The microwave has, however solved this problem to a certain extent, and this is one of the **very few Indian dishes that can be finished off cooking in the microwave.**

Recipe; Serves 3-4

Ingredients

1 glass of washed Urad daal

5-6 kari patta

1 small onion, chopped

1 inch cube of ginger cut in small thin 1/2 inch strips

1 teaspoon of ground coriander

1 teaspoon of ground cumin seeds

1/2 teaspoon of paprika

1/2 teaspoon of red chillies

1 teaspoon of salt

1 tablespoon of oil

2 glasses of water

Tarka;

1 tablespoon of ghee or butter

1 teaspoon of whole cumin seeds

1/2 small onion, chopped

2-3 small green chillies, de-seeded and cut lengthways

Pinch of red chillies

For garnishing;

5 sprigs of fresh coriander or parsley, 2-3 small, fresh, red chillies, 1 tablespoon of lemon juice

Method

(1) Wash the *daal* well, drain in a sieve and set aside.

(2) Heat the tablespoon of oil in a heavy based pan on medium heat. Fry the kari patta for 1/2 min.

(3) Add the onion and ginger and fry them till golden brown.

(4) Add the dry spices, coriander, cumin, paprika, red chillies and salt and fry for 1 min.

(5) Put in the daal and fry for 1-2 mins. Add the water and bring to the boil.

(6) Take the daal *out* of the pan and put into a deep microwave dish with a lid which allows the heat to escape. Put it in the microwave, set to medium or gentle heat and set it in for 15 mins. Take the dish out, stir with a fork and set it back in for another 15 mins. Leave it sitting for 15-20 mins to finish off cooking. Then check to see that the daal is quite dry and taste the salt Alternatively it can be cooked on low heat for the same length of time on the hob; stirring frequently with a fork so as not to break the grain.

(7) Now make the **tarka.** Fry the ghee or butter in a small frying pan on medium heat. Add the whole cumin seed and fry for 1 min. add the onion and green chillies and fry them till golden brown. Take the pan off the heat, put the red chillies in, and immediately put this tarka over the daal, before the red chillies burn out. Garnish and serve, preferably hot, but it can be served cold also.

Garnish;

With chopped coriander or parsley; set the small red chillies in the centre of the dish to give a nice colour, sprinkle lemon juice over it.

Serve;

As an accompaniment to any Indian meal; particularly good as a side dish to a meat or chicken curry.

Overall cooking time:- 45 to 50 mins

Mom's Tips

(1) Sometimes a particular batch of a daal is that of a hard variety which may take longer to cook. If you think it is not cooked at the end of half an hour in the microwave or has absorbed more water than it should, then add a few tablespoons of boiled water when necessary and set it back in the microwave for another few minutes.

(2) *Not a good dish for freezing,* as the daal does not remain crisp and dry when reheated. Otherwise the dish can be made the day before and reheated in the microwave

KALE MAAN

(Black Lentil curry);

A North Indian Daal; full of aroma; different styles of cooking it; a simple everyday daal or a rich party dish; nostalgic dish as in my young growing years Sunday lunches were associated with it because before the pressure cooker era this **daal required 3-4 hours of gentle cooking.** In the sixties and seventies a restaurant called 'Moti Mahal' in Delhi became famous for this particular daal which was made *with milk and cream, in a clay pot and served with tandoori chicken and naan and till* today I still make this combination if I am entertaining.

Recipe; ; Serves 6-7

Ingredients;

2 cups of whole Urad Daal; washed

1 med onion chopped

2 inch cube of ginger chopped

5-6 cloves of garlic chopped

1-2 green chilli chopped

1 tomato chopped

1 teaspoon of ground coriander seeds

1 teaspoon of ground cumin seeds

1/2 teaspoon turmeric

1/2 teaspoon of garam masaala

1 teaspoon salt

4-5 glasses of water

1-2 tablespoons of oil

For garnishing;

Knob of butter; 1 teaspoon of whole cumin, 2 green chilli halved; 2 cloves of garlic chopped; 1/2 teaspoon of red chilli; chopped coriander;

Method

(1) Heat the oil in a pressure cooker. Fry the onion, ginger, garlic and green chilli until golden brown. Add the tomato and fry for 1 min.

(2) Add the spices; coriander; cumin, turmeric, garam masaala salt and fry for 30 secs.

(3) Add the daal and mix well. Add 4-5 glasses of water. Close the pressure cooker lid and bring to the boil. Put the weight and from the time the whistle goes give it 5-6 mins of pressure. **Switch off the cooker and leave the cooker to sit for 1/2 hour.** *Do not attempt to open the cooker during this time.*

(4) After 1/2 hour open the cooker and mix well. Leave it on a low heat for another 30 mins. If it is too thick add water or milk or a combination of both, as much as required. Keep stirring every few mins or it will stick to the bottom of the pan. Switch the cooker off. Serve hot.

Garnish;

make the garnishing; heat the butter; fry the cumin; green chilli; garlic till sizzling. Take off the heat; add the red chilli and pour over the daal; sprinkle the chopped coriander

Serve;

best with a tandoori meat and tandoori roti or naan or with any Indian meal.

Overall cooking time:- 1 1/2 hours

Mom's Tips

(1) **Know your own pressure cooker;** it may take a few minutes more in some pressure cookers.

(2) *It is a difficult daal to make in small quantities; but it is a good dish to freeze;* before the garnishing. Make small containers so that the quantity can be finished once it is taken out. It does thicken when it cools down so add milk when reheating the dish. Add the garnish just before serving

MEHENDI or HENNA;

Traditional Art of the East

&more

Henna, or Mehendi - two words denoting the same meaning; **Henna** is an Urdu word and comes from Arabic; **Mehendi** is a Hindi word. These words conjure up the magical essence of the east; of the mystical bazaars with their roadside artists drawing intricate designs with a green paste on hands and feet of the tourists; of western newspapers and magazines linking it to temporary tattooing or even the art of doodling; of fun and celebrations at Indian and Muslim weddings.

Henna is basically a plant, green in colour; its dried leaves are crushed and made into a thick paste with eucalyptus oil.

The paste is left on wherever applied for about 4-5 hours. During that period a syrup is made with equal proportions of sugar, lemon juice and mustard oil, which is dabbed on with a cotton swab every hour or so. Although the paste is green in colour, when washed out it leaves behind hues of orange and rust. The colour cannot be washed out but will naturally fade within two to three weeks, depending on the deepness of the colour. There is a saying in India that the deeper the colour of the henna, the more love and affection the girl will receive from her mother-in-law after her marriage. If the henna paste is scraped off when dry, which is easy to do, instead of washing it off, then the colour will deepen more in the next 10-12 hours.

As it is a natural product, infact the plant has healing properties, this paste has no harmful effects on the skin, and often it leaves the skin softer then before. In the East and Middle East, this paste is also sometimes used as a hair dye, to cover the grey although the hair then gets a reddish tinge. It also softens and nourishes the hair.

Possibly because of its properties a Mehendi evening has always been a part of the festivities

The paste is left for two hours for the colour to seep out of the leaves. It is then put into a pliable plastic cone, similar to an icing cone, with which the Henna artists laboriously make patterns, generally on the palms, sometimes going up the wrists and even the arms, and on the feet, toes and ankles of the girls

The patterns are absolutely breathtaking as the artists are extremely skilful. Quite often the traditional designs means something; a lotus drawn is a symbol of purity; a coconut stands for fertility; while a peacock means passion; lace designs are for beauty. Fruits, flowers, leaves and abstract designs are intricately worked for maximum visual appeal.

leading up to an Indian wedding, more on the lines of a hen party, when the women of the house put aside a day for themselves for it amidst folk music accompanied by a two sided drum called the 'dholki'. Now the event has grown in importance; the artistic and party aspect has taken over, bollywood music has been added, men are invited and a good time is had by all. At this time, aesthetically drawn and visually appealing patterns are made on the bride's hands and feet, followed by all her friends and female relatives who in the carnival atmosphere of the evening will have a broad range of designs painted, from the most simple to the most elaborate.

My husband and I arranged a typical Mehendi evening during my son's wedding celebrations, as he was married in India. He had 25 friends from various parts of the world; Scotland, America and Australia; who came to participate. So to give them a taste of a typical Indian wedding we tried to organize a totally tradional event and hence the Mehendi evening. It started at about 2 p.m.

when the Mehendi artistes arrived. All the women of the family, aunts, cousins and friends had been invited. In one corner of the room the painting of the hands and feet went on; in another corner music was playing; in the centre some were dancing, as the boys from the family come anyway and those from abroad were invited. As the evening wore on food, wine and tea were served; the girls whose hands were painted were fed by their husbands/boyfriends. All in all, a good time was had by all. The evening ended at about 11.30 at night with the groom and his mother being the last to have the Mehendi. The groom, because he

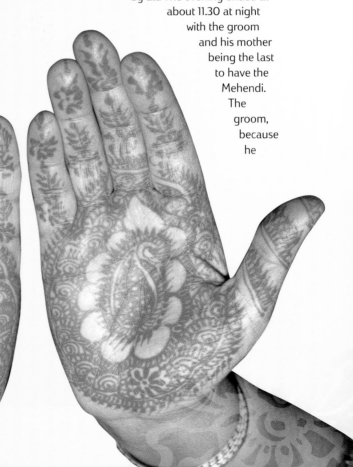

& more

one day in the year in which married women keep a total fast from sunrise to the rising of the moon in the evening for health, happiness and long life of the husband. Inherent in the Indian tradition, this one day, bindis, bangles, sindoor and mehendi, all things joyous and denoting the married state, are a big part of these celebrations. Today even birthdays and anniversaries will have the Mehendi artists working at the parties; shops and malls will have the roadside painters busy with their Mehendi cones making intricate designs on the palms of the tourists.

In the past whenever I came back to N. Ireland from my trips of India and if I had Mehendi on my palms it aroused a lot of curiosity, but the terms Henna or Mehendi were totally unfamiliar here. Then I had a lot of explaining to do.

Now with well known names in the west like Naomi Campbell and Madonna going in for Henna and its designs with a vengeance, terming it temporary tattooing, and some national newspapers carrying articles on this ancient Rajasthani' art the scene has changed. It has become fashionable in western culture with talk of beauty parlours offering the art of Henna in California, New York and London. Traditional patterns have been replaced with modern ones like cars, planes, motorbikes and dragons.

It is an enjoyable art. For those who work at the designs there is enormous pride in it as they are keeping an ancient art alive and those who get it done spend a very peaceful therapeutic hour or two while it is being done and then another 4-5 hours while nothing can be done with the hands. Possibly it is this quiet, reflective and meditative aspect that appeals to the west. Whatever it is, the interest of this side of the world has brought this art out of its hibernation and hopefully *given it a new lease of life.*

always has a dot placed in the middle of the palm for good luck and the mother, in this case me, because I was the paymaster. A brilliant evening.

Mehendi symbolizes a happy occasion. It is popular in the whole country and during most festivals; be it 'Divaali' or 'Teej' but most of all at 'Karvachauth', which is

7 SABZI, PANEER; (Vegetables and Indian Cheese);

Section

Poori Vale Aalu
(Potato curry for Pooris)

Shahi Surma Baingan
(Aubergines in spicy yoghurt curry)

Aalu Gobi
(Potatoes and Cauliflower; dry and spicy)

Punjabi Karhi
(Gram flour dumplings in a yoghurt curry)

Matar Paneer
(Peas and Cheese curry)

India is, by and large, a vegetarian country; influenced by religion and culture. Till my mother's generation these influences were very strong; the elders on both sides of my family would have been staunch vegetarians. That is *why this form of cooking must not only appear to be vegetarian but must be actually so,* **with no addition of stock or pieces of meat for flavours; only water can be added for liquid.**

The abundance of meat and poultry is limited to the north west frontier which was influenced greatly by the Muslim style of cooking food and came to be known as the **'Mughlai'** cuisine; and to the cosmopolitan cities, Bombay, Madras and Goa where the Europeans landed and made their bases. Bengal and the coastline in the south being dependent on the sea for their livelihood are fish eaters, basically because of necessity. The rest of the country was dependent on vegetables which being seasonal made them very weather dependent. Winter vegetables were always abundant, carrots, peas, turnips, cauliflower, tomatoes and salads; summer vegetables were few because of the heat and the vegetation being sparse. The two that were available the whole year were onions and potatoes. Perhaps that is why onion, nearly always makes the basis of Indian curry; or even the dry or roasted dishes and salads.

A point to note here is that, since the staple accompaniment to an Indian meal is rice or bread, potato is considered a vegetable in the Indian cuisine. Always a favourite with children particularly, it can be added to most meat, chicken or vegetable dishes for everyday meals; it can also be made into exotic dishes for entertaining. When I was a child a potato chip was a rarity and sprinkled with salt, crushed red chilli and garam masaala it was served with drinks in the evening and we were allowed to sneak a couple away; such are childhood memories!

Vegetables are the backbone of Indian cooking but there is a far greater choice in India than here where vegetables like Okra, Arbi, Sarson, or karelas, if not unheard of are sparsely available. *An Indian meal is incomplete if there is no vegetable dish on the table.* Depending on the menu the complimenting vegetable dish can be either dry, or with a sauce Nearly all our vegetables can be either dry roasted , with spices, ground or whole; or cooked with proper onion tomato masaala or even a plain yoghurt and made into a curried dish. The cooking of vegetables is an art by itself particularly since even today, with the frozen food industry being in a rudimentary form in India, we are still dependent on the seasons. This is when other vegetarian foods come into focus; lentils and pulses being one group which has been discussed in a different section; paneer being the other.

Now for the Indian cheese called **'Paneer'**. In a predominantly vegetarian country it is a very important part of the Indian food scene as being high in Protein and calcium, it is considered a substitute for meat. Made from milk, by a process in which the curds and whey are separated by the addition of something tangy, like lemon juice or vinegar or even by natural yoghurt, it produces the Indian version of a soft cream cheese which can then be kneaded and used in a variety of savouries like 'kebabs' or 'koftas' or sweets like 'rossogullas' or 'chenna-murgi'. Alternatively, the whey can be drained from the solids which are then made into a slab and when cold cut into inch cube squares or diamond shapes. It can be eaten in this form as pre-dinner snacks or fried for savouries. It can be grilled, barbecued, or added to curries. Its versatility is enormous and in fact *is the only cheese that I have come across which can be added to a curry to cook, and will still retain its shape and size and not melt.*

It is hard to find paneer in the western supermarkets among the dozens of western processed cheeses, some even unprocessed. In the sixties and early seventies when my aunt and uncle, who were vegetarians, lived in London they found it very hard to find this cheese at all, **the nearest substitute to it in its basic stage being cottage cheese.** Forty years

later the availability has not improved, although the awareness and knowledge of it has, **and now there is another substitute for it in the feta cheese.** I find it crumbly with a harder taste and would go miles to find an Indian shop for the paneer or spend the time to make it at home; for the more adventurous, I have given the recipe here.

Paneer is quick and easy to make. Bring a litre of whole milk to the boil. Watch the pan as it is easy to boil it over. Just before it boils reduce the heat; add 2-3 tablespoons of lemon juice or vinegar; stir it for 1 min. making sure that the solids and whey have separated. Take it off the heat and leave it sitting for 3-5 mins. Pour the mixture into a muslin cloth; drain the water for 10 mins; flatten the solids, still in the muslin and put a heavy weight like a saucepan with water on it to make sure it stays flat. Leave it for 2 hrs. Take out the paneer from the muslin cloth, put onto a chopping board and cut into squares or diamond shapes. You can open freeze the paneer pieces and then take out as required. I always make paneer in bulk, with about 6-8 litres of milk and freeze the pieces.

POORI VALE AALU

(Potato curry for Pooris)

A popular dish from the Panjab and Delhi regions in the North of India. Well **known for its combination with pooris, hence its name**, this dish is mild in spices and easy to make as it is one of the **rare dishes which does not have an onion masaala.** It is a good starting dish for a novice in Indian cooking. That is not to say that it is not good with rice, as my friends, who have learnt to make this dish, do serve it with boiled rice as it is quick and easy to make, as an accompaniment, and enjoy the combination. *In India, Poori vale aalu are as popular on the menus in the elite resturants as they are with the vendors and hawkers on the road side.*

Recipe; Serves 4-5

Ingredients

Method

7-8 medium sized potatoes, boiled and diced

1 teaspoon of whole cumin seeds

2 inch cube of ginger, roughly chopped

2 cloves of garlic (optional)

1-2 green chillies

2 tablespoon of fresh chopped coriander

1 small can of chopped tomatoes or 2 tomatoes finely chopped

1 teaspoon of garam masaala

1/2 teaspoon of paprika

1/2 teaspoon of red chillies

1/2 teaspoon of turmeric

1 teapoon of salt

1 tablespoon of lemon juice

1 glasses of water

3-4 tablespoons of oil

For garnishing;
5 sprigs of fresh coriander, chopped, pinch of garam masaala, pinch of chaat masaala or amchur

(1) Make a paste of the ginger, garlic, chilli and fresh coriander and set aside.

(2) Heat the oil in a heavy based pan. Fry the cumin seeds for 1 min.

(3) Add the paste from above and fry for 1min. Then add the can of tomatoes and fry for another 2 mins.

(4) Now add the dry spices, garam masaala, paprika, red chillies, turmeric, and salt and fry for 1 more min.

(5) Put in the diced potatoes and mix thoroughly. Add the water; mix well again, do not worry if the potatoes are getting a little mashed as that will thicken the gravy. Cover the pan and bring to the boil, reduce the heat and simmer for 15 mins. Switch off the heat and check the thickness of the curry. Add the tablespoon of lemon juice; taste the salt; garnish and serve hot

Garnish;
With fresh chopped coriander, sprinkle garam masaala and chaat masaala or amchur

Serve;
With pooris, boondi raita and kachumbar salad; or with boiled rice, green salad and garlic bread.

Overall cooking time:- Boiling and preparing potatoes 30 mins, making curry 30 mins.

Mom's Tips

(1) *If you prefer you can substitute 2 fresh tomatoes for a can of tomatoes.* I use the can in this particular dish as it gives a nice red colour to the dish which does not come with only fresh tomatoes.

(2) Not a good dish for freezing as the potatoes do not retain the fresh flavour of this curry when defrosted.

SHAHI SURMA BAINGAN

(Aubergines in spicy yoghurt curry);

A dish with a hint of **Mughlai** form of cooking; it was experimented and made for a group of friends who wanted something totally different; it was a great success and has been often repeated for small and large gatherings as it is fairly easy to make in large quantities. It is exotic enough for my young son to make it in his flat in Australia for his friends; the same son and I made it in open competition at a fair in London and competed against a chicken dish and this won for its taste, simplicity and cost efficiency,

Recipe; Serves 3-4

Ingredients

1 large aubergine sliced

1 small green pepper cut into rings

1 small red pepper cut into rings

1 med red onion sliced or in rings

Yoghurt curry;

1 cup of natural yoghurt

1 tablespoon of lemon juice

1 tablespoon of tomato ketchup

1 green chillies, deseeded and cut lengthways

1 teaspoon of whole cumin seed

1 teaspoon of ground coriander seeds

1 teaspoon of ground cumin seeds

1 teaspoon of ground fenugreek seeds

1/2 teaspoon of red chillies or paprika

3/4 teaspoon of salt

Oil for frying

For garnishing; 2 green chillies; 2 red chillies; sprigs of coriander

Method

(1) Heat the oil in a broad based frying pan. Fry the aubergine slices in batches and set aside on kitchen paper to absorb the oil. Do the same with the pepper rings and the onion slices. Arrange these in a shallow serving dish with the aubergines as the bottom layer, then the peppers, finishing with the onions.

(2) Mix the lemon juice, tomato ketchup and the salt with the yoghurt and set aside.

(3) Heat 1 tablespoon of oil and fry the cumin seed and the green chillies till sizzling. Add the ground spices coriander, cumin, fenugreek and chillies and fry for 30 seconds. Switch off the heat. Add the yoghurt mixture and stir well. Pour over the arranged vegetables. Reheat in the microwave; garnish and serve hot.

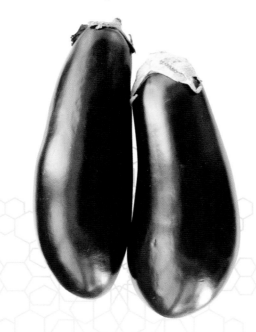

Garnish;

Sprig of coriander in the middle, with the whole chillies on the side of it

Serve;

with rice, naan or as a side dish to meat or chicken; with any Indian meal

Overall cooking time:- 35-40 mins.

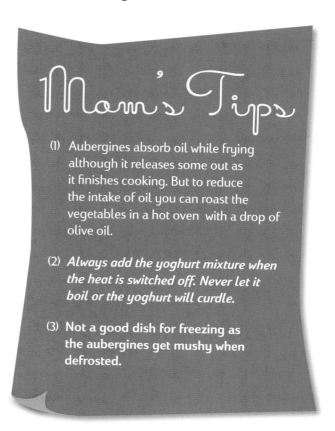

Mom's Tips

(1) Aubergines absorb oil while frying although it releases some out as it finishes cooking. But to reduce the intake of oil you can roast the vegetables in a hot oven with a drop of olive oil.

(2) *Always add the yoghurt mixture when the heat is switched off. Never let it boil or the yoghurt will curdle.*

(3) **Not a good dish for freezing as the aubergines get mushy when defrosted.**

AALU GOBI

(Potatoes and Cauliflower; dry and spicy)

A very traditional north Indian 'generally' an everyday dish; a firm favourite of my husband; simple to make and easy to gather up the ingredients for. I have used the word 'generally' quite deliberately as it can be converted into a party dish; but to make a dry dish in a large quantity can be a daunting task on a domestic hob in which case the technique can be varied slightly, given below, which makes it into a more exotic dish.

Recipe; serves 4-5people

Ingredients

1 med cauliflower washed and cut into bite sized florets

3-4 med potatoes, washed; skinned; diced

1 inch cube of ginger, finely chopped

1 small green chilli finely chopped

1 tablespoon of fresh coriander chopped

1 teaspoon of whole cumin seeds

1 teaspoon of ground coriander seeds

1 teaspoon of ground fenugreek seeds

1/2 teaspoon of turmeric

1/2 teaspoon of red chillies or paprika

3/4 teaspoon of salt

2-3 tablespoons of oil

For garnishing; chopped fresh coriander, garam masaala

Method

(1) Heat the oil in a wok or a deep frying pan on a med heat. Add the whole Cummin seeds and fry till sizzling. Add the potatoes and fry for 2-3 mins add the cauliflower florets and mix well. Now add the chopped ginger and green chilli.

(2) Add all the spices; coriander, fenugreek, turmeric, chilli and salt. Mix it well; sprinkle a tablespoon of water and cover the pan. Reduce the heat slightly. Stir lightly **every 5 mins to make sure it does not stick to the bottom of the pan.**

(3) Cook for approximately 15-17 mins. Switch the heat off but leave the pan sitting on the warm hob to *finish off cooking in the steam.*

Garnish;
arrange on a platter or a shallow dish, sprinkle with chopped coriander and garam masaala.

Serve;
With any Indian meal as a side dish; particularly good with 'Kale maan,' 'Karhi' or 'Rogan josh'

Overall cooking time:- 25 - 30 mins.

Mom's Tips

(1) *Cauliflower is easy to overcook* so always undercook it slightly and let it finish in its own steam.

(2) If you like the **skins left on the potatoes**, especially. new potatoes, it makes a tastier dish.

(3) The dish can be made a few hours in advance, microwave and then garnished just before serving. **Not a good dish to freeze.**

Variation

(1) Using a *Chip fryer fry the cauliflower florets* in batches and set aside. Deep fry the **potato cubes and set aside.**

(2) Heat 1 tablespoon of oil on med heat fry the whole cumin seed, ginger and chilli for a few seconds. Add the rest of the dry spices. Add the fried vegetables. Mix well Cover and cook for 2-3 mins on low heat. Switch off the cooker and leave for 10 mins for the flavours to mix.

PANJABI KARHI

(Gram flour dumplings in a yoghurt curry)

A firm favourite of north India, particularly Panjab, Uttar Pradesh and Rajasthan where Karhi and rice is as famous as fish and chips in Britain or chilli con carne in Mexico; an unusual dish as the base is yoghurt and gram flour which give it a distinctive taste of its own. Some would say it is an acquired taste. In early seventies when Indian food was relatively unknown here, the mention of Karhi would bring our Indian friends from across Belfast on a moments notice.

Recipe; Serves 3-4 people

Ingredients

Batter for the dumplings;

1 cup of gram flour sieved

1/4 teaspoon of baking soda or baking powder

1/4 teaspoon of salt

1/4 teaspoon of chilli or paprika

1 tablespoon of fresh chopped coriander

1/2 cup water, approximately

Oil for frying

Yoghurt curry;

1 cup of yoghurt

3 cups water

2 tablespoons of gram flour sieved

1/2 teaspoon of turmeric

1/2 teaspoon of paprika

1/2 med onion chopped

1 inch cube of ginger chopped

4 cloves of garlic chopped

2 teaspoons of ground fenugreek seeds

1 teaspoon of ground coriander seeds (optional)

1/2 teaspoon of salt

2 tablespoons oil

For garnishing;

knob of butter; 1 teaspoon of whole cumin; 2 green chillies halved, pinch of red chillies; chopped fresh coriander

Method

(1) First make the batter. Mix the gram flour, baking soda, salt, chilli and fresh coriander with 4-5 tablespoons of water till the batter has a dropping consistency.

(2) Heat the oil in a wok or a deep frying pan on a med to high heat. Drop half a tablespoon of the batter at a time in the oil and fry the round balls for 3-4 mins. Make in batches. Depending on the size you should get 12-15 balls.

(3) Whisk the yoghurt, water, gram flour, turmeric and paprika and set aside.

(4) Heat 2 tablespoons of oil in a saucepan, Fry onion, ginger, garlic and green Chilli until golden brown. Add the ground fenugreek, coriander and fry for 20 secs. Add the yoghurt mixture and stir constantly till it comes to the boil. Reduce the heat and let it simmer for 12-15 mins. Or until the curry is thickened. Add the dumplings and then take it off the heat and let it sit for a few mins.

(5) Prepare the garnish. Heat the butter; fry the whole cumin seed; take off the heat and add the red chilli.

Garnish;

Heat the dish; pour the warm garnish over it; sprinkle the chopped coriander.

Serve;

with boiled or onion rice and an onion and green chilli salad

Overall cooking time:- 1 hour.

Mom's Tips

(1) **You can add chopped onion and finely diced potatoes or both, to the batter** for the pakora balls.

(2) Be careful when you add the yoghurt mixture as there is *danger of the Yoghurt curdling so keep stirring till it boils.*

(3) Fenugreek seeds are very important in the recipe for the distinct taste to the curry important

(4) If it is too thick add a few spoons of boiled water

(5) Not a good dish for freezing

Variation

If you do not have the time to make the dumplings, sauté diced mixed vegetables; potatoes, carrots, turnips and even peas. Add these to the yoghurt curry at the same time as the dumplings.

MATAR PANEER

(Peas & Cheese curry);

A North Indian dish, this is probably the **most popular of the cheese dishes**, available in the smallest of cafes and in the best of restaurants. A simple dish, easy to make, it has great fascination here, as firstly the **cheese remains firm, does not melt with the heat; and secondly the availability of frozen peas** not only makes the dish accessible the year round but also takes away the labour of shelling peas. A treat for the vegetarians as the cheese is considered a substitute for meat.

Recipe; Serves 4-5

Ingredients

Cheese of 1 litre of milk, (the recipe for this given earlier) or 250gms of paneer (commercial variety)

1 cup of frozen or shelled peas

1 large onion, roughly chopped

1 inch cube of ginger, roughly chopped

4-5 cloves of garlic

1-2 green chillies

3-4 sprigs of fresh coriander, washed

1 small can of tomatoes or 2 fresh tomatoes, finely chopped

1/2 teaspoon of ground coriander seeds

1 teaspoon of ground cumin seeds

1 teaspoon of ground fenugreek seeds

1/2 teaspoon of paprika

1/2 teaspoon of red chillies

1/2 teaspoon of garam masaala

1 teaspoon of salt

1- 1 1/2 glasses of water

3-4 tablespoons of cooking oil

For garnishing;

5 sprigs of fresh coriander, chopped, pinch of garam masaala

Method

(1) **First prepare the cheese.** Cut the paneer into diamond shapes, about 1 inch wide and 1/4 inch thick. Then heat 4 tablespoons of oil in a non-stick frying pan and shallow fry the paneer pieces on low heat. Be careful when frying as paneer browns very quickly; it will take 1 min. for each batch to become golden in colour. Set aside.

(2) Put the onion, ginger, garlic, chilli and coriander leaves in the food processor and chop finely. Set aside.

(3) Heat the oil in a heavy broad based pan and fry the chopped ingredients of the onion masaala, till golden brown. This should take 5-6 mins.

(4) Add the dry spices, coriander, cumin, fenugreek, paprika, red chillies, garam masaala, turmeric and salt and fry them for 1 min.

(5) Add the tomatoes, and fry for 1 min.

(6) Put in the peas and fry for 2-3 mins; if fresh peas increase the time to 5mins

(7) Add the water, bring to the boil and reduce the heat. Drop in the paneer pieces, mix well, cover the pan and let it simmer for about 15-20 mins. Switch off the heat, check the thickness of the curry; taste the salt; garnish and serve

Garnish;
with chopped fresh coriander and sprinkle garam masaala.

Serve;
with any Indian bread, or boiled rice, a dry daal or any side vegetable, a yoghurt or raita and an onion and tomato salad.

Overall cooking time:- 40-45 mins; making the cheese 30 mins.

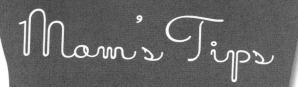

Mom's Tips

(1) You can substitute 2 fresh tomatoes for the small can of chopped tomatoes, although I think that the can gives a better colour to the dish.

(2) Cutting the paneer into diamond shapes is conventional; but they can be cut into squares or rectangles, as long as, roughly, the thickness and the size remains the same.

(3) The dish can be frozen, but the paneer does seem to lose some its fresh taste when it is frozen in a curry. It can be reheated in the microwave.

DAHI and LASSI
(Yoghurt and Buttermilk);

Section 8

Boondi Raita
(Yoghurt with small Gram flour fritters)

Kheere ka Raita
(Yoghurt with grated Cucumber)

Kachumbar Raita
(Yoghurt with Onions, Tomatoes, Cucumber & Peppers)

Aalu Raita
(Yoghurt with Potatoes)

Dahi-Gurgullas
(Yoghurt with Lentil fritters)

Laal Anaar ka Raita
(Yoghurt with Pomegranate seeds)

Yoghurt, commonly known as *'dahi'* is an *essential* in Indian food; a necessary must in North Indian and Bengali food. **It is an accompaniment that is not just cooling in taste but its herbal properties counteract the spices making it good for digestion also**. It can be added to curries at the cooking stage to make variations in dishes; or it can be added to chutneys like mint or coconut.

It is a very versatile item; it can be had as plain natural yoghurt, the way it is set, as it is generally eaten with an everyday meal; or it can be whisked slightly and have different ingredients added; boiled potato, chopped salad; or grated cucumber and made into a sort of relish called 'raita'. Long before the fruit yoghurts or petit filous came into the market this natural yoghurt was had with sugar, jaggery, jam, syrup and eaten as a sweet.

It is the main ingredient in an exotic, tangy and very spicy form of a group of **Indian snack food called 'Chaat', particularly a dish in it called 'paapri chaat'** It has chopped boiled potatoes, chopped onions, boiled chickpeas, dahi bade and paapri, which are made from plain flour and taste like fried tortillas. All these are piled onto a plate and the whisked salted yoghurt poured over them with as much or as little spice and chaat masaala as you want over it and a touch of the tamarind and mint chutneys with it. *The taste of this dish is very local and very Indian.*

It can be made into a **summer drink called 'lassi'** and with plenty of ice it is one of the nicest drinks to have in a hot summer's afternoon as it has no fizz in it. It can suit all tastes as it can be had as it is, bland; with salt or with sugar. The forerunner of this drink was 'Chaach', a well known drink in the Panjab;

it was the buttermilk left in the churns after the butter was made; in India it has a different taste to it as the milk used was buffalo milk; the cream of which was set like yoghurt and then churned. Milk is now substituted for cream, the butter is eliminated and only the drink is made. The younger of my twin sons comes home in the summer months especially to drink this, as, of course he is a bachelor and lacks the expertise to make the yoghurt; he is convinced that the English buttermilk which is the closest to our lassi, does not even come close to it, in the matter of taste. Of course he could be biased.

Dahi; It is very easy to make yoghurt. The difficulty is to get non bio yoghurt to start making yoghurt with. If you can get it then; boil half a pint of milk; put it in a glass bowl; cool it down to a temperature that it should feel hot to the touch; put 1 tablespoon of yoghurt in it; cover it and set it in a warm place for 8-10 hours to let it set. Do not move it again. **The three tips** in this are; **always boil the milk** and then cool it otherwise the yoghurt will not set; *the warm place is essential* for the culture to work in setting the yoghurt; **use 1 tablespoons of the same yoghurt for the next day's yoghurt.**

'Lassi'; an easy drink to make; put a glass of yoghurt and an equal measure of water in the liquidizer with 4-5 cubes if ice and churn for 1-2 mins. If serving bland take it out now and serve. Otherwise add sugar or salt and churn for another 30 secs and then serve. If you serve it with salt you can add a pinch of garam masaala, or pinch or ground dry roasted cumin and a sprig of mint.

BOONDI RAITA

(Yoghurt with small Gram flour fritters)

A very traditional north Indian dish, equally popular in the Panjab and Delhi regions although even the south of India now has a variation of it; versatile, as it can be part of any everyday meal or dressed up as a party dish. I have written the recipe for this dish from the basics, which includes the fritters or the boondi because in the eighties when I first came here there was no commercial variety for it available. To cut down on the work involved my friends experimented with rice krispies in place of fritters as that is what the appearance of the boondi is but it was not a success. Now you can get bags of boondi in the deli or Indian shops which can be put in the freezer and taken out when required; this would eliminate the first part of the recipe. **To make the boondi you need a flat frying steel round spatula with holes in it as it is through these holes that the batter will** *fall into the hot oil to make the fritters.*

Recipe; serves 4-6

Ingredients

Method

Batter for Fritters;

1 cup of gram flour

1/4 teaspoon pf baking powder

1/4 teaspoon of salt

1/4 teaspoon of paprika

1/2 cup of water approximately

Oil for frying

For Raita;

2 cups of yoghurt

1/2 teaspoon of salt

1/4 teaspoon of red chilli or paprika

1/4 teaspoon of garam masaala

2 tablespoons of water

For garnishing;

1 teaspoon of ground dry roasted cumin seed; sprigs of mint; pinch of red chillies

(1) Sieve the gram flour in a mixing bowl; add the baking powder, salt, paprika; make a batter with the water till it arrives at a loose dropping consistency. Let it sit for 10 mins.

(2) Heat the oil on a medium heat. When hot, hold the flat steel spatula over the oil and put the batter on the spatula and set it fall through the holes, you can use the back of a spoon to hurry the process. It should take just a few seconds; Keep turning them over with another slotted spoon; they should be cooked and golden brown in 1-2 mins. Take them out and leave them on kitchen paper to drain the excess oil while you finish making the rest of the batter in the same way.

(3) Put these in warm water for 4-5 mins; then drain the water and squeeze all the water out of the boondi with your hands and put them in a serving bowl.

(4) Whisk the yoghurt; add the salt, red chilli or paprika, garam masaala and water and mix thoroughly. Pour over the boondi and mix well. Keep in a refrigerator to keep cool till you are ready to serve.

Garnish;

sprinkle the ground dry roasted cumin and red chillies on the dish and arrange the sprigs of mint;

Serve

with any Indian meal; particularly with pooris and potatoes.

Overall cooking time:- 30 mins to make the fritters; 10 mins to make the raita

Mom's Tips

(1) Children **like the taste of boondi itself as it is crisp and dry**; it is good as a snack or with drinks.

(2) *It can be frozen at the end of step two;* take out as much as you require; the boondi can go straight into warm water for step three,

KHEERE KA RAITA

(Yoghurt with grated Cucumber);

An Indian meal is never compete without a plain natural home-made yoghurt called dahi or its variations called raita, which are generally salty. This dish is one of the variations; it is a cool, summer dish; it can be had as an accompaniment to a simple meal or part of a set buffet; I have also seen it being used as a dip for crisps and carrot sticks and it has been just as much appreciated. Although the home-made dahi has a lovely flavour of its own, but if you do not have the time to make it, this dish can be made with any of the commercial varieties of natural yoghurt.

Recipe; serves 4-5

Ingredients

1/2 cucumber

1 cups of natural yoghurt, homemade or commercial

1/2 teaspoon of salt

1/4 teaspoon of garam masaala

For garnishing;
Chopped bits of the skin of the cucumber, pinch of ground roasted cumin, pinch of red chillies

Method

(1) First prepare the cucumber. Grate it with skin on, squeeze the water out of it and set it aside in the bowl in which you are going to make the dish.

(2) Whisk the yoghurt, add the salt and garam masaala and pour it over the grated cucumber. Stir gently with a fork. Keep it in the fridge till you require it. Garnish it just before serving it.

Garnish;
Arrange the chopped cucumber on the dish; sprinkle the ground roasted cumin and the red chillies.

Serve;
With any Indian meal or as a dip.

Overall cooking time:- 15 mins

Mom's Tips

(1) Cucumber has a lot of natural juices in it; so you must squeeze it before making the raita or the dish will be very watery.

(2) Not a good dish for freezing.

KACHUMBAR RAITA

(Yoghurt with Onions, Tomatoes, Cucumber & Peppers)

Since **an Indian meal is not complete without yoghurt,** the different ways it can be served are interesting; it can be unusual like the aubergine and mustard seed raita; it can be exotic like dahi-bhallas; it can be with starters as in chaat; it can be in chutneys as in mint or coconut chutney; or it can be very simple, with universally known salad ingredients as have been used in this raita; the word 'kachumbar' *meaning finely chopped and mixed food.* A favourite of my family, every evening if possible; this is actually a summer dish as these salads are summer produce and mixed with yoghurt are very cooling in the hot season.

Recipe; Serves 4-5

Ingredients

1/2 cucumber; cut into small chopped pieces

1 medium red onion; chopped into small pieces

15-18 small cherry tomatoes quartered

1/2 green peppers chopped into small pieces optional

1/2 yellow peppers chopped into small pieces, optional

1 1/2 cups of yoghurt, home made or commercial

1/2 teaspoon salt

1/2 teaspoon garam masaala

For garnishing;
red chilli or paprika; sprigs of mint or chopped fresh coriander

Method

(1) Mix the cut ingredients and put them in a serving bowl; set aside.

(2) Whisk the yoghurt with salt and garam masaala; pour over the chopped salad and mix well. Garnish and serve cold.

Garnish;
sprinkle red chilli just before serving; arrange 2-3 sprigs of mint in the centre of the dish;

Serve;
serve with any Indian meal

Overall cooking time:- 10mins.

Mom's Tips

(1) **Not a dish to freeze** It can be made well in advance and refrigerated as it is served cold.

(2) **You can omit making a salad with the meal** if serving this raita or have just the salad leaves with salt pepper and lemon juice in them

AALU RAITA

(Yoghurt with Potatoes);

Another variation of the yoghurt dish, particularly popular in the Panjab; this variation is a favourite of children as it has potatoes in it and that is a universally liked food item. It is not dependent on the seasonal produce as the 'kachumbhar' raita or the 'Kheera' raita are; it is easy to gather the ingredients for and quick to make unlike the 'Boondi' raita; and has a traditional appearance. It can be made for a family meal or a party with equal success.

Recipe; 4-5 people

Ingredients

3-4 medium Potatoes

2 cups of yoghurt, homemade or commercial

1 teaspoon salt

1/2 teaspoon of garam masaala

Pinch of red chilli

3-4 tablespoons of water

For garnishing;
Pinch of red chilli; pinch of ground dry roasted cumin seed; sprigs of mint;

Methad

(1) Boil the potatoes; cool them; peel them; dice them in small pieces; roughly mash a couple of pieces; Put them in a serving bowl and leave them aside to cool

(2) Whisk the yoghurt, salt, garam masaala, red chilli and the water. Pour it over the potatoes and mix well. Serve cold.

Garnish;
sprinkle the red chilli, garam masaala, cumin and arrange the sprigs of mint;

Serve;
with any Indian meal

Overall cooking time:- 25-30 mins.

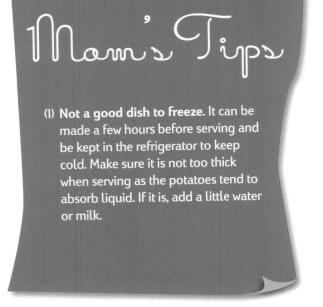

Mom's Tips

(1) **Not a good dish to freeze**. It can be made a few hours before serving and be kept in the refrigerator to keep cold. Make sure it is not too thick when serving as the potatoes tend to absorb liquid. If it is, add a little water or milk.

DAHI-GURGULLAS

(Yoghurt with Lentil fritters);

A very popular north Indian dish; part of the 'Chaat' group of foods which are served spicy and with tangy chutneys, tamarind and mint. The chaat is part of our very culture and so inherent in our day to day life that every small market, any street with shops; any fairs or 'melas' as they are called, will have chaat corners; small or big restaurants will have chaat on the menu; wedding dinners will have chaat stalls. ***One of the main dishes of chaat is dahi-gurgullas,*** *which can also be served on their own as a side yoghurt dish;* it used to be a party dish because of the time it took to make the fritters but now with the freezers in the kitchens it has become easier to make these days in advance and freeze them

Recipe; makes 25-30 gurgullas depending on the size

Ingredients

Method

For the gurgullas;

2 cups washed Moong lentil

4 cups of water

1 teaspoon salt

1/2 teaspoon baking powder

1 tablespoon of chopped fresh coriander

Oil for frying

For the raita;

2-3 cups of yoghurt

1 teaspoon of salt

1/2 teaspoon garam masaala

3 tablespoons of water

For garnishing;

pinch of red chilli, pinch of ground dry roasted cumin, chopped mint

(1) Wash the Moong daal well. Soak in the 4 cups of water and leave overnight.

(2) Drain the water and put the daal in the food processor with 1-2 tablespoons of water and process it into a thick batter. It will take 2-3 mins.

(3) Put the batter in a mixing bowl and mix vigorously till the batter is light; takes 5-6 mins. Add the salt, baking powder and chopped fresh coriander.

(4) Heat the oil in a wok. When hot add a tablespoon of batter and see the round ball which should float up. Put 9 to 10 at a time; turn them over and let them cook for 2-3 mins. or until golden brown. Put them on kitchen paper and let them drain while you finish making the rest of the batter the same way.

(5) Whisk the yoghurt, salt, garam masaala and the water; set aside.

(6) Soak the gurgullas in warm water for 5-6 mins; then drain them and squeeze the water out of each gurgulla with the hand till it is quits dry but soft. Arrange these in a shallow dish or a platter.

(7) Pour over the yoghurt mixture making sure that all the gurgullas are covered and there is extra liquid in the plate as the gurgullas will soak it. Clingfilm the dish and keep in the refrigerator; serve it cold

Garnish;

sprinkle red chilli, roasted ground cumin, arrange chopped mint.

Serve;

Serve with tamarind and mint chutney; accompaniment to any Indian meal; also with paapri chaat

Overall cooking time:- 45 mins.

Mom's Tips

(1) To make the *gurgullas* soft and crispy **it is very important to mix the batter with energy in step** (3), to make the **gurgullas** more spicy add finely chopped ginger and green chilli in the batter

(2) **Not a good dish to freeze. *The gurgullas can be frozen after step*** (4); defrosted when required and then the rest of the dish can be made

LAAL ANAAR KA RAITA

(Yoghurt with Pomegranate seeds);

A modern variation of a yoghurt dish; made with a fruit it has a sweet tinge with the savoury taste. Particularly liked here in the western world where even a little bit of spice sometimes can feel hot. It was made by chance for the first time in our house when I was trying to make something different but mild with a touch of sweetness for my group of friends, two of whom were scared to try any spices at all; but this colourful dish gave them the courage to try the rest; and they were converted. *A slight touch of ginger and chilli gives it a zing in the taste.*

Recipe; 4-5 people

Ingredients

1 pomegranate

1/2 cube ginger, finely grated (optional)

1/2 green chilli finely chopped (optional)

2 sprigs mint, finely chopped

1/2 teaspoon chaat masaala

1/2 spoon salt

2 cups yoghurt

For garnishing; pinch red chillies; pinch chaat masaala; mint sprig

Method

(1) Deseed the pomegranate. Mix the seeds with the ginger, green chilli and mint. Add the chaat masaala and salt. Set aside.

(2) Whisk the yoghurt. Add the pomegranate mixture. Mix well. If too thick add one tablespoon of water,

Garnish;
sprinkle red chillies and chaat masaala put the mint sprig in the middle.

Serve;
With any Indian meal, particularly if there is a very hot dish

Overall cooking time:- 15 mins.

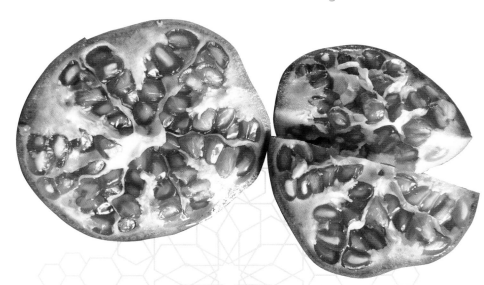

Mom's Tips

(1) Not a good dish to freeze.

Chaaval
(Rice)

Pyaz Pulao
(Rice with Onion)

Meat Biryaani
(Rice with Lamb Meat)

Matar Pulao
(Rice with Peas)

Navratan Pulao
(Exotic vegetable Pulao)

Gobi Pulao
(Rice with Cauliflower)

Section 9

Rice is possibly the most versatile grain, or staple food that I have come across. **It can be cooked plain, with vegetables, with meat, with chicken, with lentils, with or without spices, sweet or savoury;** just about anything to suit different tastes. It comes in **two different forms;** *the square rice,* a variation of which is the Patna rice, another the American long grain rice. This variety is heavy on starch, is good for boiling only, as the rice has to be boiled in a large volume of water, and when cooked the water has to be drained which takes a lot of the flavour away, although it leaves the grains dry and separate. This rice is popular in South India and Eastern India which is the Bengal province; both have boiled rice as their staple food. The second variety is the Indian long grain rice, well known as Basmati rice, which is the favourite of North India. It grows best in the foothills of the Himalaya Mountains of India and Pakistan; has slim long grains which have a flavour of their own and is by far the most expensive of the rice.

My recipes generally use Basmati rice. Once you have learnt the technique to cook this you will possibly never go back to any other variety, not just because of its taste but because of its sheer cooking simplicity as the Basmati will turn out perfect every time.

Some points to note about the basmati rice; *point one;* due to its low content of starch, **this is the only rice which will absorb all its water while cooking,** leaving the grains fluffy, dry and separate. This also means that you must follow the proportion of rice and water meticulously to achieve the best results, as less water would leave an edge to the grain, more would make it soggy. In my recipes, I use two measures of water to one measure of rice. *But then I also wash the rice just before cooking it.* This is a very important point because you might read other recipes where the proportion of water might be less than mine, but in those you might find that rice has been washed half an hour in advance and left soaking in the water, in which case the grains

would have absorbed some of the liquid. So do follow whatever recipe you are following completely, including the washing instructions. Do not mix and match. This is particularly important when following the recipes on the variations of rice where various spices, herbs, vegetables, meat or chicken may have been added to the rice, as the total absorption of water ensures the total retention of the flavours within the dish. Generally, when there are spices and vegetables added to the rice it becomes a *'Pulao',* when meat or chicken is added it is called *'Biryaani'.*

Point two; Use a heave based pan with a good fitting lid. Always bring the rice to the boil on high heat, then reduce the heat and **partially cover** the pan, never fully, or it will boil over. After half the required cooking time cover it fully and leave it like that for the rest of the time.

Point three; **resist the urge to peep into the pot of rice** once you have switched the cooker off as the last bit of cooking is really done in the steam, and lifting the lid would release the steam and then the rice will not be evenly cooked.

Point four; rice is a delicate grain particularly after it has been washed. When you fry the rice at the start as most of my recipes will say do it very gently or the grains will break up. If you want to give the rice a stir halfway through before closing the lid fully, do so with a fork. When serving the rice at the end of the cooking do so with a flattish large slotted metal spoon, again gently, layer by layer and fork it through to separate any grains stuck to each other. Traditionally, and for parties, rice is served in a flat oval dish.

Point five; As I have said before, we do not use stock, particularly in our vegetarian dishes therefore these rice dished will be based on water. If you prefer, you can substitute chicken stock for water in the same volume.

In the days before the electric hobs and cookers, when cooking was done on the coal fires, I remember my mother cooking rice in a very innovative way. As she could not regulate the heat from the bottom

of the pan, she would close the lid tightly once the water was reduced, then take the pan off the heat, put a heavy Iron griddle on top of the flat lid and place a few burning coals on it. The weight of the griddle kept the steam in longer, and the coals on top gave it a low heat to finish off the cooking. The result, needless to say, was perfect every time.

It is very easy to boil basmati rice with little effort; wash 1 cup of rice; add two cups of water; Put it on high heat on the hob and bring it to the boil; Watch it as it is easy to boil over. As soon as it comes to the boil, lower the heat, half cover the pan and let it simmer for 10 mins. Stir it with a fork lightly so as not to break up the grains; fully cover the pan tightly; leave for another 2-3 mins. Switch off the cooker and leave it sitting with the lid closed for 10 mins to allow the grains to finish cooking. Serve it in the saucepan to let it stay as warm as possible. Electrical rice cookers are also a good idea; they cook the rice to perfection; they keep it warm for a length of time; it then can be used to serve in style as well.

PYAZ
(Rice with Onion);
PULAO

A popular form of rice in India, especially good for parties because of its **enchanting brown colour.** It is a form of rice that can be ***cooked all year round*** as onions are always available; it's a form of rice that can be cooked to **accompany most dishes,** possibly any dish as there are really no strong flavours in it. Remember to wash the rice just before cooking and not leave the rice soaking in the water or it will upset the ratio of the liquid while cooking.

Recipe; Serves 4-5

Ingredients

2 glasses of Basmati rice

1 large sized onion, thinly sliced

1 spoon of black cumin seeds

2 black cardamoms split

4-5 cloves

1 stick of cinnamon, an inch long

3-4 bay leaves

2 level teaspoons of salt

4 glasses of water

3-4 tablespoons of cooking oil

For garnishing;
2-3 rings of fried onions and 2 fresh bay leaves if available

Method

(1) Wash the rice well, drain and set aside.

(2) Put the cooking oil in a heavy based pan and heat on medium heat. Fry the onion rings to a golden colour and keep aside for garnishing.

(3) Add the cumin seeds, cardamoms, cloves, cinnamon and bay leaves, and fry for one min.

(4) Then add the onion slices and fry until they are really dark brown.

(5) Add the rice and fry for 1 min.

(6) Put the 4 glasses of water and bring to the boil.

(7) Reduce the heat, partially cover the pan and simmer for 7 mins. Then open the lid, gently stir with a fork and then fully close the lid and cook for another 7-8 mins. (total of 14-15 mins). Turn the heat off and leave the pan sitting without opening the lid for another 8-10 mins. Garnish and serve, preferably hot, although it can be had cold also. It should be light brown in colour in its finished state because of the fried onion leaving its colour in the water while cooking.

Garnish;
With the rings of fried onions and the fresh bay leaves.

Serve;
With any curry, meat or vegetable, but is particularly nice with kidney beans or rogan josh. A good party dish because of its colour.

Overall cooking time:- 35 mins

Mom's Tips

(1) The onions must be very deep brown in colour, nearly black, as it is the onions that will give out their colour in the water to give the finished rice its lovely light brown colour.

(2) If black cumin seed is not available you can use the ordinary cumin seed instead.

(3) Again, as for the rest of the rice dishes, not good for freezing. Reheat on a flat dish in the microwave and the grains should become fluffy again.

(4) The rest of the tips are the same as for all rice dishes as in the general discussion on rice at the start of this section.

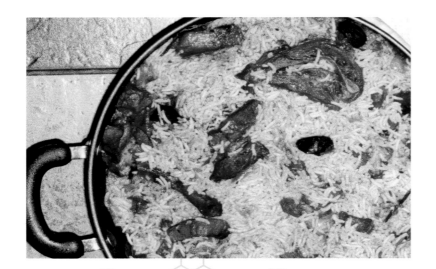

MEAT (Rice with Lamb Meat); BIRYAANI

A North Indian dish, adapted from the rich spicy non-vegetarian Afghan cuisine, **this is a great party dish as it is a complete meal by itself.** A big plate of hot Biryaani set in the centre of a table accompanied by a couple of yoghurt dishes, a salad or two and a variety of pickles is all that is required to look inviting and festive. A firm family favourite, the secret of this dish is to have plenty of meat and onions in it. There are many different ways of making a Biryaani; with mutton; with chicken; with pheasant; the Hyderabadi way; the Mughlai way; the Afghani way; but this is a quick and easy method and can be made with ease, even for a novice at Indian cooking.

Recipe; Serves 5-6

Ingredients

Method

For the Meat;

1 kg of lamb meat, preferably leg or shoulder, cut into 1 - 1 1/2 inch cube pieces with the bone

1 teaspoon of black cumin seed

4-5 bay leaves

2 black cardamoms split

2 green cardamoms split

3-4 cloves

1 stick of cinnamon an inch long

10-12 peppercorns, coarsely ground

1 medium sized onion, chopped

1 inch cube of ginger, finely chopped

2-3 cloves of garlic, chopped

1/2 tomato, chopped

1 small green chilli, finely chopped

1 teaspoon of ground coriander seeds

1/2 teaspoon of ground cumin seeds

1/2 teaspoon of paprika

1 teaspoon of garam masaala

1/4 spoon of turmeric (optional)

1 teaspoon of salt

3-4 tablespoons of oil

To finish the Biryaani;

2 glasses of Basmati rice

1 teaspoon of salt

4 glasses of water

For garnishing; 4-5 sprigs of fresh coriander, chopped, and half an onion sliced and fried

(1) Put the oil in a heavy based pan and heat on medium heat. Add the black cumin seed and fry for a few seconds till they sizzle. Add the bay leaves, cardamoms, cloves, cinnamon and black peppercorns and fry for 30 secs.

(2) Add the chopped onion, ginger and garlic and fry until golden brown. Then add the tomatoes and green chilli and fry till the juices have dried and the oil can be seen in the pan.

(3) Now add the dry spices, coriander, cumin, paprika, garam masaala, turmeric and salt and fry for about 30 secs

(4) Put in the meat and mix well. Fry on the medium heat for about 8-10 mins, again mix well, lower the heat and let it cook in its own juices for another 30 mins. Stir it every few minutes to make sure that it has adequate water of its own in which to cook; if it looks less add a few spoons of boiling water. The meat should be nearly cooked at the end of 40 mins and have a thick sauce at the bottom of it. At this stage the oil should also be seen at the bottom of the pan.

(5) Add the rice and mix well. Put in another teaspoon of salt, add four glasses of water, mix again and bring to the boil on a high heat. Then lower the heat, partially cover the pan and let it simmer on low heat for 7-8 mins. Open the pan, stir lightly with a fork, close the lid tightly and let it cook for another 5-6 mins. Switch off the heat and let the pan sit with the lid closed for about 10 mins. Then taste the salt, gently lift the rice and pile it onto a broad serving dish, garnish and serve hot.

Garnish;

with the fried sliced onions and chopped coriander.

Serve;

with a yoghurt dish, a green salad and a mango or lime pickle; with any Indian meal; a party buffet dish.

Overall cooking time:- 1 hour and 20 mins.

Mom's Tips

(1) **The bone in the meat gives an extra flavour to the dish** and if you have a good butcher, he will chop it for you. *But, if that is not possible then you can still make the dish with just meat pieces. If you prefer pork or beef pieces you can use them instead.*

(2) Make sure that there is no water left in the meat before you add the rice or the proportion of the water to the rice will get affected and the grains then may not be as fluffy as they should be.

(3) **The meat can be made the day before a party** and the rice can be added about an hour before the meal is to be served as it takes just the same length of time to cook it as it would take to reheat it.

(4) It is a good dish to freeze also, but after step (4) when the meat is cooked. Defrost it, add the rice and finish off the Biryaani. Do not freeze the cooked rice as I have found it to become soggy when defrosted. If you need to reheat, do so in the microwave.

MATAR PULAO

(Rice with Peas);

In India this form of rice is very popular; a bit of a delicacy as peas is a winter vegetable, and keeping in mind that India relies on seasonal vegetables and not the frozen food industry, **this form of rice can only be made for 3-4 months in the year.** We are more fortunate here in the west with the frozen peas, but even so, the taste and fragrance of **_this dish with fresh shelled peas is distinctly better._** The rice should be washed just before you start cooking otherwise the grains will absorb water and the ratio of the water to the rice will not remain accurate.

Recipe; Serves 4-5

Ingredients

2 glasses of Basmati rice

5-7 strands of saffron (optional)

1 cup of frozen or fresh shelled peas

1 teaspoon of cumin seeds

2 black cardamom split

3-4 cloves

1 stick of cinnamon, an inch long

2-3 bay leaves

2 level teaspoons of salt

4 glasses of water

2-3 tablespoons of cooking oil

For garnishing;

sprig of fresh mint or a sprig of fresh parsley or a couple of fresh bay leaves if available

Method

(1) Wash the rice well, drain and set aside.

(2) Soak the saffron strands in two tablespoons of warm water.

(3) Heat the oil at medium heat and fry the cumin seeds, cardamom, cloves, cinnamon, and bay leaves for one minute.

(4) Add the peas and fry for 2-3 mins.

(5) Add the rice and salt and fry for 1-2 mins.

(6) Put in 4 glasses of water and bring to boil. If you are adding the saffron then add it at this stage.

(7) Reduce the heat, partially cover the pan and simmer for 7 mins.

(8) Lift the lid, very gently separate the grains with a fork, tightly close the lid and leave for another 7 mins.

(9) Switch off the cooker and leave the pan without opening the lid for at least 8-10 mins before serving. The finished dish should have an off white colour with a hint of yellow; garnish and serve hot.

Garnish;

with a sprig of mint, or parsley and, or, the fresh bay leaves.

Serve;

with any curried dish, particularly good with a lentil. Can also be served on its own with pickles and plain yoghurt.

Overall cooking time:- 30 mins.

Mom's Tips

(1) **If using fresh peas then add on a couple of extra minutes** when frying them in step (4).

(2) If you like carrots, then add half a gated carrot to the dish when the water is added, as it will enhance the looks and flavour of the dish.

(3) If you do not have saffron and would still like some colour in the dish you can add a pinch of turmeric, although it will be a stronger colour. Or you can omit this ingredient and still enjoy the dish.

(4) Again not a good dish for freezing as rice tends to become soggy when defrosted, but if made in the morning, take care to reheat in the microwave only.

(5) For the rest of the tips see the general discussion on rice at the start of the section.

NAVRATAN PULAO

(Exotic vegetable pulao)

A party dish with a touch of the mughlai form of cooking, this was very popular in my parent's house when they were entertaining. Since my mother learnt this dish from a friend who was called 'Shankla' this dish has always been referred to as 'Shankla pulao' in our house and my mother has won many a cooking prize for this easy yet exotic form of rice. **A touch of panache about it** as it is best when the grain, though properly cooked should not be sticky which in the case of rice is easily done; so my mother would have finished off the cooking by taking it off the heat; which was either coals or gas; and then put a heavy griddle or tava on top of the saucepan; sometimes with a couple of hot coals on it; to keep the steam in the pan to finish off the cooking.

Recipe; serves 5-6 people;

Ingredients

2 glasses of rice

1 teaspoon of whole black cumin seed

2 inch stick of cinnamon

5-6 cloves

2 green cardamoms split

4-5 bay leaves

1 med onion sliced

1 carrot cut into matchstick size pieces

4-5 florets of cauliflower, cut into smaller pieces

1/2 cup of fresh peas

4 glasses of water

6-8 strands of saffron

10 small pieces of fried paneer

10-12 **almonds sliced**

1-12 **cashew nuts halved**

20-25 raisins

1 teaspoon of salt

4 glasses of water

3-4 tablespoons oil

For garnishing;
chopped almonds; a few pieces of fried paneer; chopped fresh coriander

Method

(1) Wash the rice; drain and set it aside

(2) Heat the oil in a saucepan. Fry the black cumin, cinnamon, cloves, cardamoms, bay leaves for 30 secs or until they sizzle. Add the onion and fry for 1 min; add the carrot, cauliflower and peas and fry on a gentle heat for 3-4 mins.

(3) Add the rice and mix well. Put the heat up to high. Add the water and the saffron strands. Bring it to the boil uncovered; reduce the heat to low; half cover the pan and let it cook for 12-14 mins; Halfway through the cooking add the dry fruit; almonds, cashew nuts and raisins and paneer pieces and stir them through the rice with a fork so as not to break the grains of rice; then cover tight with a lid and leave it for the remainder of the time

(4) Switch off the cooker; do not open the pan for 10 mins during which time leave it sitting on the warm hob; serve hot.

Garnish;
decorate with the chopped almonds and the paneer; sprinkle coriander.

Serve;
Rice can be served in the saucepan in which it is cooked or in a platter; with pickles, chutney and a green salad; with any Indian meal or buffet.

Overall cooking time:- 30-35 mins.

Mom's Tips

(1) **Wash the rice just before cooking** or it will affect the ratio of the rice and water which is very important in rice cooking.

(2) **Not a good dish for the freezer** as the rice gets soggy when defrosted; but it can be made a few hours in advance and then reheated in a platter in the microwave, which leaves the rice fluffy again.

(3) **The rest of the tips are the same as for all the rice dishes as in the general introduction at the start of this section**

GOBI PULAO

(Rice with Cauliflower);

A dish from North India, it **is a good party dish because of its golden colour; it does not need much accompaniments** as it already has a vegetable in it, a vegetable that most people will like. Very popular in India as again cauliflower is a winter vegetable and available for a limited time period only. In the west it can be made throughout the year as cauliflower seems to be on the shelves of the supermarkets the whole year round. Wash the rice just before you cook it; do not leave the grains in water or they will soak in the water and upset the quantity of water at the cooking stage.

Recipe; Serves 4-5

Ingredients

2 glasses of basmati rice

4 glasses of water

1 small to medium sized onion, sliced in rings

1 small cauliflower, washed and cut

1 teaspoon of black cumin seeds

1-2 small green cardamoms split

4 cloves

1 stick of cinnamon, an inch long

4 kari patta

10-12 peppercorns

1 teaspoon of salt

3-4 tablespoons of cooking oil

For garnishing;
A couple of florets of fried cauliflower, a fried ring of onion, 1 bay leaf

Method

(1) Wash the rice well and drain in a sieve and set aside.

(2) Heat the oil in a heavy and broad based pan and fry the ring of onion and a couple of florets of cauliflower to a golden brown. Set aside for garnishing.

(3) Add the cumin seeds, cardamoms, cloves, cinnamon, bay leaves and black peppercorns and fry for 1min.

(4) Add the onion rings and fry them until they are dark brown.

(5) Add the cauliflower pieces and salt. Mix well. Cover the pan and cook for 3-4 mins stirring occasionally.

(6) Add the rice and fry it gently for 1 min.

(7) Put in the 4 glasses of water and bring to the boil.

(8) Reduce the heat, partially cover the pan and simmer for 8 mins. Uncover the pan, stir the rice very gently with a fork, fully cover the pan, and cook for another 7 mins. Turn off the heat and leave the pan without opening the lid, to finish off the cooking in its own steam. Garnish and serve hot.

Garnish;
With the fried florets of cauliflower, onion rings and the bay leaf that have been kept aside.

Serve;
Can be served with any curried dish, but particularly good with chickpeas curry. Again a good party dish because of the brown colour of the rice. It can also be served on its own, with a mango pickle and a yoghurt dish.

Overall cooking time:- 35 mins.

Mom's Tips

(1) For this rice a skillet or a broad based pan with a tight fitting lid is ideal.

(2) Remember to make the onions really dark brown to enable to give out its colour in the water, which will eventually give the rice its lovely brown colour.

(3) If you do not like the crunch of the whole black peppercorns, as my family does not, then you can coarsely crush the peppercorns before adding them.

(4) Again, this dish is not good for freezing as rice tends to become soggy when defrosted. Reheat in the microwave in a flat dish.

(5) For the rest of the rice tips, do read the general discussion on rice at the start of this section.

THE SARI

Draped in tradition

&more

Women love clothes; women from *all over the world* love clothes; women from *anywhere in the world* love clothes. They love to buy them, wear them, criticize, admire them and if the clothes are at all different, with an aura and a mystic around them, they fascinate them. The *Sari*, the dress of the east has these facets and more. It comes in fabulous colours, is worn in a mysterious style, and although Indira Gandhi, a past Indian Prime Minister, glamorized it on the international scene through the seventies and the eighties, it was the fact that Cherie Blair wore it to an Indian event that made the headlines in the national press, and has made it accessible to the women here with the thought; it may be from the east, but it could be worn successfully here also.

The sari is a dress that is ageless; old but traditional saris, woven with pure gold and silver threads called *'Tilla'* and *'Zari'* are preserved in muslin cloths and soft tissues and handed down from mothers to their daughters, to be worn, possibly once in five years and then packed again. Bridal saris, generally red in colour, are worn on the occasions of other weddings in the family, as long as the particular shade of red does not clash with that of the bride, and then passed on to the next generation.

It is a versatile dress. For the elite and the rich, the fabric can be *silk or brocade* for the winter months, or *organza, chanderi or voile* for the hot summer; for the middle class or the poorer section it would be thick *cotton or fine muslin,* but whichever, it can be dry-cleaned, washed, starched or ironed, depending on the material and worn to perfection.

The **colours of our saris are breadth-taking;** generally **bold** is the theme; magenta pink, turquoise blue, rainbow purple, sunset orange, emerald green; you name the colours we have them all. Traditionally, white and black as colours were not worn; the reason behind it being; white is the colour of mourning in India; and black would be too strong

Saris with hand embroidery of Kashmir, the *'Kandha'* stitching of Bengal, the *'Chicken'* work of Lucknow are examples of the versatility of the craftsmen which have become well known internationally.

Well known for its silk, the variety of it in India is staggering. The brocades of Banaras in the north, is actually silk interwoven with gold and silver thread; the silk from Bengal is firm and thick, with white and red being their traditional theme; Gujarat silk is as famous as that of Banaras, with more emphasis on thread work than on gold and silver, and during the Mughal times was well known for its velvets also; the silk from the south is thick with a lovely shine and is produced in most colours, bright and subdued, of which the variety of 'Kanjivaram' is the most popular, but the Mysore silk and the Bangalore silk have a soft feel which is in a category of its own. The raw silk of Assam traditionally known as 'Tussar' silk is well known internationally.

As an outfit, the Sari is timeless; there is no stitching involved; its hem does not go up or down, it is always worn to fall to the floor. That is why it is a difficult dress to wear in Britain on a day to day basis because of the wet weather, as I found to my cost when I first arrived in Britain twenty five years ago. *It is six yards long and one and a half yards wide* material; it can be totally plain, or totally patterned, or it can have a three to four inch border on both the edges and a matching wide border, sometimes as wide as a yard, at the end of the sari which falls from the shoulder. This is called the **'Palla'** or an **'Aanchal'** I am not suggesting that patterns and colours do not change with the changing colours of the seasons or the years; they do. I could recognize a particular style or colour of a *Patola* or a *Baatik* as that of the early eighties. But in due course, colours come back and the saris are dry-cleaned and brought back into circulation, and with a new blouse and new petticoat the outfit looks glamorous again.

and absorb too much heat which makes it an unfit colour for a hot country, but keeping in tune with today's modern international colour scene both the shades have crept in.

The designs range from the floral to hunting scenes, - to motifs of creepers, figures of birds and animals to modern abstract or block designs. The better known designs are the *'Baatiks'* of Bengal and the *'Baandhini'* and *'Leheria'* of Rajasthan, which are the products of tie and dye technique, and have caught on to the imagination of the west also. Then there is the *'Kalamkari'* or the printing technique from Andhra Pradesh which represents mythology and religious scenes, the traditional *'Patola'* from Hyderabad with block style designs or just contrasting borders, plain but effective from the south.

The sari has become a topic of conversation on more than one occasion; whether it is the rarity of the dress, the vibrant colour or the three inch bare midriff even if it is loosely covered with sari! Today in the progressive India and the bollywood dress styles, saris are being worn with off shoulder blouses which are designed like bikini tops!

When I give my evening talks to women's groups or mothers unions it invariably ends up with the topic of my sari; is it really only a long piece of material tucked in here and there;

is it definitely not stitched or pinned; how is it worn? Some of the answers to the above questions are given below. For the rest, read the inset.

A point to note here is that saris can be worn in at least a dozen different ways; southern India have their own way of draping a sari; Parses brings the palla round to the front; Bengalis wear saris which are nine yards long. Below is the most popular version, internationally known as the Indian sari.

How to wear a traditional Sari;

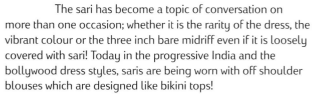

Before you start to wear a Sari make sure of three things; firstly, have a full length petticoat in a matching colour; preferably the petticoat should be in a cotton fabric and have a full skirt; secondly, have a blouse to match the sari, not too long, just long enough to leave two to three inches to the petticoat; and last but not least, attach a fall to the bottom end of the sari. This fall is generally a cotton fabric about three to four inches wide, three yards long, and is attached to half the length of the sari starting from the inside end.

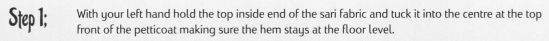

Step 1; With your left hand hold the top inside end of the sari fabric and tuck it into the centre at the top front of the petticoat making sure the hem stays at the floor level.

Step 2; Making sure that the hem stays at the same level at the floor, wind the material round the waist coming back to the front and making sure it is tucked into the petticoat all round.

Step 3; Now start making pleats, till about the last two yards of the material. You should be able to get 6-8 pleats. Tuck these in the petticoat also, again at the front still making sure that the hem stays at the same level.

Step 4; Now wrap the remaining material around yourself once more and let the surplus hang over your left shoulder.

Step 5; If necessary pin the pleats together to the petticoat on the top where they start. Put another pin or preferably a broach on top of the left shoulder, holding the top end of the sari with the blouse.

Roti, Naan aur Paranthas
(Indian Bread)

Poori
(Deep fried Roti)

Tandoori Roti
(Grilled wholemeal bread)

Roomali Roti
(Wholemeal thin chapaathi; shallow fried)

Naans
(Grilled white flour bread)

Bhaturas
(Deep fried plain white flour Rotis)

Section 10

An Indian meal of meat and vegetables cannot be eaten on its own; it must be accompanied by either some form of rice or, any style of bread, or a combination of the two. It also depends on where you live in India as; the southern and eastern areas are rice growing and consequently rice eating provinces; while the fields in the north grow the wheat which makes the inhabitants there extremely skilful in making different types of breads for their daily consumption.

Rice is discussed in a different section; now the bread. The most important point to note here is that it is different to the bread in the west as *it is unleavened.* For most of the Indian breads it is not a complicated process to make the dough as there is no yeast in it to necessitate the sitting and rising time. The **dough is made, just with flour and water**, ready for use immediately. That is why our bread is made fresh before every meal, and contrary to belief, does not take much time. A word here about the flour to use; the best would be the *'Chapaati flour;'* or **'Atta'** as it could be referred to in the Indian shops where it would be available. If you are unable to get this then make your own by mixing half of plain flour and half of wheaten and then kneading it into dough.

Indian bread is very versatile. It can be simple; *'Chapaathis,'* or as we call them 'Phulkas' in the Panjab, are made on a griddle; '*Tandoori Rotis'* are grilled; **'Paranthas'** are shallow fried; **'Pooris'** are deep fried; **'Naans',** which are possibly the most well known in the west are partially different, as they are made with plain flour for a start and then have yeast added to the dough. Each type is delicious, especially

if the particular bread is matched with the dish it goes best with; Pooris with Channas, Naans for meat dishes, Paranthas with pickles and raitas. Rotis or Paranthas can be plain, or they can be stuffed with; either grated cauliflower; or dry roasted lentils; or even just chopped onion, green chillies and coriander. When stuffed with mashed potato it reminds me of the Irish potato bread.

You will need a flat cooking utensil to cook most of these breads. In India we have a flattish, cast iron concave shaped griddle called a *'Tava',* which is ideal. It is available in Indian supermarkets. If you are unable to obtain one you can use a large heavy based saucepan or even a griddle on which you bake soda bread, even though it is totally flat. To deep fry Pooris you will need a heavy based Balti-cum-Wok type of a utensil called a *'Karaahi'.* Again if you are unable to get one, though I have seen them in large supermarkets, use a Wok or a deep frying pan, but be careful not to fill it more than 1/4 as oil as it does tend to splash out when you drop the Pooris in.

I make fresh Chapaathis every night before we sit down for our main meal, generally two per person. The number can be decreased if there is rice as well or it can be increased if there are youngsters on the table, particularly boys. On a Sunday I would make Pooris, guaranteed to cause overeating, and the number can be confidently increased to 3-5 per person, depending on the size of the Pooris.

The process of making these breads is fast and interesting and fascinates children. I first learnt to make these, starting with the Chapaathi, when I was

ten years old, so it cannot be a difficult art. Once you have learnt to make them you will never enjoy the pre-packed variety of the stores again.

When I first went to work in Northern Ireland in Hospital administration, and went to the canteen for my lunch I was most mystified to see only meat, vegetables and potato on my plate. I could not see any bread with the meal. The girls at the counter could not understand why I would need it, and would not sell me a roll without any soup. So I used to end up with two meals on my plate. Today, of course, the food display in the same canteen is totally different; Potatoes, rice and rolls are all available, with any meal, or even on their own.

POORI

(Deep fried Roti);

Equally popular in the North and South of India, and in fact even in the East, although their version is slightly different, the Poori is one of the tastiest and most versatile of the Indian breads. **Children will roll it up and have it just plain**; a great party bread once you have mastered the technique, as they are very quick to make; they can be made into a combination with any Indian dish, dry or curried, although the most well known combination is with a potato curry which is called 'Poori wale Aalu'; or they can be had with sugar and jam. They can be made plain or with a slight hint of spinach, mint, potato or even lentil.

Recipe; Makes 15-20 Pooris

Ingredients

1/2 kg of Chapaathi flour, or a mixture of wholemeal and plain flour

1 teaspoons of cooking oil

Pinch of salt

1 cup of water (200-250 ml)

Oil for deep frying

For garnishing;
leaves of fresh coriander

Variation

The most popular variation is with a hint of spinach. Add 2-3 tablespoons of cooked and pureed spinach in step (1) with the water, reducing the water content with the same amount. It should give a green colour to the dough.

Follow the rest of the steps from the recipe; the pooris should have a shade of green colour and slightly different taste.

Method

(1) Put the flour in the mixing bowl; add the salt and one teaspoon of cooking oil to it. Then with a dough hook, make the dough by adding water slowly. Add just as much as required and no more, as the dough must be firm.

(2) Heat the oil in a Karaahi or a Wok, on a high heat.

(3) While the oil is heating, divide the dough into 15-20 portions and make smooth round balls with each.

(4) Grease a rolling board, preferably one of marble. Also put one teaspoon of cold cooking oil in a dish by its side. Take each ball, dip the edge of it in the oil, set the round on the rolling board and roll it out to about 4-5 inches in diameter.

(5) When the oil is hot, drop the poori in and fry for about 30 seconds on each side, or until golden brown. Lift out with a slotted spoon and drain on kitchen paper. Make all the pooris the same way; spread them out on a flat dish or a basket, garnish and serve. Make about 3-4 per person, more if there are youngsters, less if there is rice also.

Garnish;
Conventionally the Pooris are not garnished. However, if you want to do so sprinkle a few leaves of fresh coriander on them.

Serve;
With any Indian curry or dry dish; especially well known with Channas, or Poori vale Aalu.

Overall cooking time:- 45 mins.

Mom's Tips

(1) **The dough should be really firm** to be able to roll on a greased board. If it is still difficult to roll as it does need practice then you can roll out with plain flour. The reason for rolling it with the oil is that the oil remains clean till the end of frying, while the plain flour tends to burn in the oil and this burnt residue then tends to stick to the subsequent pooris.

(2) Make the round balls first and then start rolling out. With practice you will be able to fry a poori and roll out the next at the same time. If need be, all the pooris can be rolled out at the start, before you start frying, but they do tend to dry a bit if you do too many at a time.

(3) If you do not have a Karaahi or a Wok, us a frying pan with deep sides making sure that the oil does not splash out when you drop the pooris in.

(4) *Make sure the oil is at the right temperature.* When hot, drop a small piece of dough into the oil. If it floats to the surface and turns light brown immediately, the oil is at the correct temperature

(5) The pooris will be filled with air as soon as they are taken out of the oil but they will flatten out very quickly as the air escapes.

(6) **Very good for freezing.** They can be stacked and frozen and taken as required. Not good for reheating in the microwave, as they tend to dry out. Reheat lightly under a grill.

TANDOORI ROTI

(Grilled wholemeal bread);

Indian bread from North India, the Tandoori Roti is particularly a favourite of those from the Panjab region. As the name suggests, ***it was originally made in the Tandoor or the clay oven*** and still is done so in restaurants and hotels but at home it can be partially made on a griddle and then finished off under the grill. Generally served at parties and dinners as it is always considered more exotic than just a plain Chapaathi or bread. This recipe is for the plain roti and not for the exotic layered variety which can be complicated

Recipe; Makes about 10-12 Rotis

Ingredients

1/2 kg of chapaathi flour, or a mixture of wholemeal and plain flour

1 cup of water (200-250 ml) approximately

2-3 tablespoons of chapaati flour or wholemeal flour

For garnishing;
I teaspoon of ghee or melted butter and a few leaves of fresh coriander

Method

(1) Put the flour in the mixing bowl. Then adding the water slowly make a firm dough with the dough hook, cling film the dough and keep in a cool place till required, possibly in the fridge.

(2) Put the Tava, which is an iron cast griddle, on a high heat. If a tava is not available use a heavy based non stick frying pan.

(3) Shape the dough into 10-12 round balls. Then, sprinkle some plain flour on a rolling board; roll one ball out with a rolling pin to about a diameter of 5-6 inches, using more plain flour if needed.

(4) Put this round on the tava to cook. This one side should take about 1 minute to cook. Do not cook the other side just take it off the tava and keep warm in a tea towel. At the same time roll out the next roti and have it ready to put on the tava. Make all in this way and stack them in the tea towel.

(5) Put the grill on at full heat. Set two to three rotis on top of the wire mesh in the grill pan with the uncooked side on top. Brush with milk and set under the grill. It should become golden brown in about 2 mins. Take them off, brush them with the ghee or the melted butter, stack them again in the tea towel and keep hot while the rest are finished cooking the same way. Garnish, and serve immediately, while still hot.

Garnish;
with melted butter and leaves of fresh coriander

Serve;
Best with the whole black lentil dish called Kaale Maan; also good with any meat, chicken, or tandoori dish. Can be served with any Indian curry.

Overall cooking time:- 35-40 mins.

Mom's Tips

(1) The dough is best used on the day it is made; however it is still usable for the next day if kept in the fridge.

(2) It is best to roll out the *rotis* as you are making them. However, if that is difficult, roll out about four at a time, make those and then roll out some more. Too many rolled out and left sitting tend to dry them out.

(3) The *rotis* can be half made; till the end of step (4); and left stacked in a tea towel for 1-2 hours and then when the meal is nearly ready to be served they can be set under the grill to finish off cooking.

(4) **If cutting down on fat they can be had without the ghee or butter** and will still taste excellent.

(5) Good for freezing, particularly at the half cooked stage; at the end of step (4). Stack and freeze them; take out as many as required, defrost slightly, brush them with milk and cook them under the grill. Do not defrost the rotis fully or leave them sitting out for too long as they tend to become slightly deeper in colour and lose their fresh look.

ROOMALI ROTI

(Wholemeal thin chapaathi; shallow fried)

A variation of the basic Indian bread roti, this has a more exotic style to it as it is made with two layers. Made in the Mughlai School of cooking this roti, traditionally had several very thin layers; legend has it that in an old restaurant in Agra, the heart of the Mughal capital, **there was a chef who made it with a hundred layers; the connoisseurs have counted them.** A good bread if entertaining, as it can be made an hour before serving and kept well wrapped up; double insulated containers are good for keeping them warm.

Recipe; Makes 18-20 roomali rotis

Ingredients

3 cups of chapaathi flour, or half wholemeal and half plain flour

1-2 cups of water

2 tablespoons of chapaathi flour for dusting the rotis when rolling them

3-4 tablespoons of oil

For garnishing;
sprigs of coriander

Method

(1) Sieve the flour in the food processor bowl and make a dough by putting the water through the top; Use as much as required or when the dough looks 'made' leaves the sides of the bowl and feels firm to the touch. Cover with a damp cloth or with cling film and set it aside.

(2) Heat the tava or a griddle or a heavy non stick frying pan on high heat.

(3) Divide the mixture into 18-20 small balls and leave them on a greased tray; cover with a damp cloth

(4) Dust the rolling board and roll out one ball of dough thin, to a diameter of 10-12 inches, using the dry flour if necessary. Set aside

(5) Roll the second one to the same size; spread a touch of oil on the surface of one round and put the second one lightly on top of it. Do not seal the edges as the rounds will have to be separated once they are cooked.

(6) Put the two rounds together on the hot tava; cook for 30 secs. Turn it over and cook for 40 secs. Apply 1/2 teaspoon of oil on each side as you turn it over and cook each side again for 30 secs on each side or until it is golden brown is colour.

(7) Bring the cooked roti off the heat and separate the two halves. Fold each separately and make each into a triangle. Keep both rotis warm while you finish the rest in the same way. Serve hot.

Serve;
Put the sprigs of coriander on the rotis; with any Indian meal; particularly with meat and chicken dishes.

Overall cooking time:- 30-35 mins.

Mom's Tips

(1) **Amount of water varies** because each form of flour will absorb a different quantity; so do not put all the water at once, adjust accordingly

(2) In step (4) be careful as the oil is put in between the layers so that they so not stick with each other and that is why **it is important not to press on the edges as it is easy to seal them**

(3) *Using butter when frying on the tava gives the rotis a better taste*

(4) **Not good to freeze** as they are difficult to reheat.

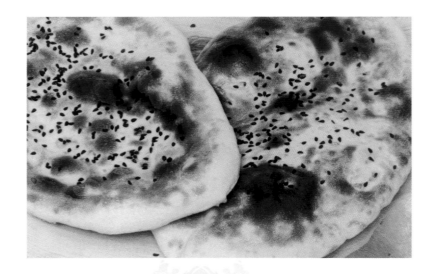

NAANS

(Grilled white flour bread);

   Possibly the most popular of Indian breads, the naan is a product of the north, or rather the north-west, an adaptation of the rich Afghan cuisine. That is why it is best accompanied by rich **Mughlai** dishes like *Shahi Murgh, Meat korma or a Murgh Mussalam.* There are a variety of naans, depending on the ingredients added; there could be plain naans with a sprinkling of onion seeds or sesame seeds; or there could be garlic ones; or garlic and coriander; but the most famous of them are the Peshaavri naans which are rich in their constitution, difficult to have too much of, but extremely tasty. **The home made naans are far lighter in texture than the commercial varieties and as they are easy to make they are well worth the effort.** Below is a recipe for 'home made' plain naans; it is a quick to make recipe as I have used self raising flour, instead of the traditional method of using yeast to make the dough, and I think the results are just as good with less effort.

Recipe; Makes 12-15 naans.

Ingredients

1/2 kg of self raising flour or plain flour with 1 teaspoon of baking powder

2 tablespoons of cooking oil

1/2 teaspoon of salt

2 cups of buttermilk or homemade natural yoghurt

3 tablespoons of milk

1 tablespoon of onion seeds

2 tablespoons of melted butter

For Garnishing;
fresh chopped coriander

Method

(1) First make the dough. Sieve the self raising flour in a bowl with the salt. Add the 2 tablespoons of oil. Add the buttermilk or the yoghurt little by little as required and make a soft dough. Then oil your hands, lift the dough out, make it into a nice round ball, set it back into the bowl, cover it with a wet muslin cloth to prevent it from drying, and set it in a warm place for 5-6 hours.

(2) Oil your hands and then divide the dough into 12-15 small round balls. Then grease your rolling board and roll out each ball into an oblong shape, about 8 inch long and 3 inch wide. Set aside.

(3) Heat a tava or a heavy based frying pan on a medioum heat. Place a naan on the tava and cook for about 1 min. In this minute keep checking the underside to see if it is golden brown. Once light brown slide it off the tava and set it on a grill tray with the uncooked side facing upwards. Make another 2-3 naans the same way or until the grill tray is full.

(4) Put the grill on at high heat. Brush the tops of the naans with milk. Then sprinkle some onion seeds on each naan and slide the grill tray under the hot grill and cook for about 1-2 mins, checking all the time. When brown take them out, brush them with melted butter and keep them warm in a tea towel until all the naans are made in the same way.

Garnish;
Traditionally there is no garnish as the melted butter is already brushed, but you could sprinkle chopped fresh coriander to give it a party look.

Serve;
With any Indian meal; particularly good with any meat, chicken or a paneer dish and a yoghurt and an onion salad on the side.

Overall cooking time:- 10 mins to make the dough and 45 mins to make the naans.

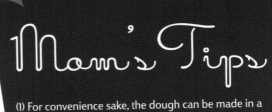

Mom's Tips

(1) For convenience sake, the dough can be made in a food processor.

(2) The hot press is an ideal place to keep the dough in for it to rise, as it is just warm and not too much so, as sometimes even a low oven might be.

(3) As the naans cook quickly *make sure the tava or frying pan is not too hot, although the grill should be at high heat.*

(4) Ideal for freezing. Make batches, put cling film or greaseproof paper in between each, making it easier to take as many out as required. Reheat under a medium grill.

BHATURAS

(Deep fried plain white flour Rotis)

A popular form of bread in the Panjab and Delhi, bhaturas and channas combination with the tamarind chutney can be **a Sunday lunch; for entertaining; or in a restaurant.** You can never go wrong in its choice; for the young or the elderly; even though it is a rich form of bread as it is deep fried, but its temptation is enormous. The original version of making bhaturas was laborious as it involved fresh yeast but I have simplified it by using the dried variety.

Recipe; Makes 8-10 bhaturas depending on the size

Ingredients

1/2 kg of plain flour

1/2 teaspoon level salt

1 teaspoon sugar

1 teaspoon dried yeast

1/2 cup warm milk

1 cup warm water

Oil for frying

Method

(1) Sieve flour; salt; sugar together. Add the yeast. Add the warm water and milk and make into smooth dough. Cover with a damp cloth and leave in a warm place for the bread to rise; leave for 4 hrs; knead again; leave for another 1 hr.

(2) Divide the mixture into 8-10 balls. Cover with a damp cloth and leave them sitting on a greased tray.

(3) Heat the oil. Roll out the bhatura on a greased surface; thin and to a diameter of 7-8 inches; test if the oil is hot by putting in a touch of the dough, it should sizzle immediately; gently put the bhatura in and fry for 30 secs on one side and 30 secs on the other side; lift out and keep on kitchen paper till the others are made. Serve hot

Serve;

with 'channas' and tamarind chutney; 'Poori vale Alu' and mint or mango chutney are the best combination; or with any Indian meal.

Overall cooking time:-

10 mins to make the dough; 30 mins to finish the cooking

Mom's Tips

(1) Because of the yeast, the **dough will spring back a little** when rolling it but persist with the rolling and it will fry perfectly alright.

(2) **Bhaturas are quick to make; easy to overcook;** if two people are working together, one to roll and the other to fry then it is easier and quicker to make them.

(3) **Good to freeze;** put greaseproof paper in the middle of each so you can take as many out at a time as required; **Heat under the grill** as the microwave will dry them out.

MISHTAAN

(Indian Sweets and Deserts);

Gulaab Jamuns
(Deep fried fritters in golden syrup)

Kulfi, Zafrani Badaam Pista
(Indian ice-cream with Saffron,
Almonds & Pistachios)

Kheer
(Indian rice pudding)

Sooji ka Halva
(Desert with Semolina)

Besan ki Burfi
(Sweet squares made with Gram flour)

Section 11

As I have said elsewhere in this book Indians do not go overboard on deserts. That is not to say they do not have a sweet tooth; they do. *But it is not mandatory to have a sweet every night; if it is served at a family meal, it is a treat.* For a house party, two sweets would be an average number. So dishes which would fit the conventional use of the term of sweets, as in an after dinner trolley, the range would be limited. Some of the popular deserts today in this category were originally inspired by different religious sects as these were made as offerings and then offered to the congregation at the end of a service. *'Kheer'*, a form of rice pudding was made by the Hindus; *'Sooji ka halva'*, a dish made with semolina was made popular by the *Sikhs*; *Sevian'* or *Vermicelli* was served at the Muslim gatherings. All three are excellent in taste, the origination is generally forgotten and they are served as pure deserts. In addition, a mention must be made of the most popular of the North Indian sweets, **'Gaajar ka halva'**, which is made with grated carrots, sugar and butter. Eaten hot or cold, it is a very seasonal, winter sweet. Summer time would bring in ice-cream or *'Kulfi'* with its Indian flavours; cardamoms, pistachios, saffron or mango; or natural yoghurt with sugar or "Shakkar" which is unrefined brown sugar, for any time of the year

Indian sweets and deserts are essentially the same. They can be served at any time; for elevenses, teatime, just snack or after dinner. The pastry like 'Indian sweets', which are sold in sweetmeat shops in India, or under glass counters and pre-packed boxes in the Indian stores in Britain, are collectively called *'Mithai'.* This is a very big industry in India. Perhaps it is unfair to compare it to pastry, which is either a cake or a biscuit base, where as Mithai has a solidified milk base. Again a difficult art to muster if made in the traditional manner, where the milk has to be boiled down to its solids. This is a lengthy, time consuming process, but the Indian chefs who make these sweets and are called **'Halvais'**, have this know-how passed down to them from generations and are adept at it. The variations of this are enormous; we have **'Burfi'**, made with the milk solids, but with different flavours and colours; with almonds it can be off white; with coconut it can be pink; pistachio could make it green, and saffron would make it yellow. The other two well known sweets, whether in the east or the west are; **'Gulaab jamuns'**, which are, as an Irish friend of mine once said, very much like syrupy doughnuts; and **'Rasogullas,** is a very popular Bengali sweet, made with Indian cheese and a touch of semolina.

These are all milk products as generally all sweets are. But milk being in short supply in the shops in the summer months these products are taken off the shelves. This fact makes it all the more interesting in the west where the ingredients are always available. The downside is that the whole process is lengthy and tedious therefore shortcuts are devised and now, quite often, condensed milk or dried milk is used instead of boiling down the milk to the solids as I have done in some of the following recipes.

My friends here in the west would say that Indian sweets are too 'sweet'; perhaps it is an acquired taste as I, who does not have a sweet tooth and would not have meringues or cheesecakes for the same reason, would love to have a 'rossogullas' or a 'Kulfi' whenever I go back to visit Delhi

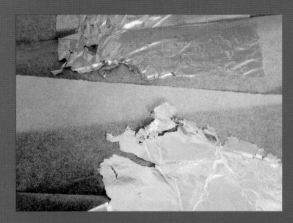

GULAAB JAMUNS

(Deep fried fritters in golden syrup);

Very popular with adults and children; a great favourite of my whole family; there is no English name for this North Indian sweet. Described as 'syrupy doughnuts' it is a *very versatile sweet, as it can be had at any time of the day; for elevenses, afternoon tea, or as a desert.* As a boarder in the halls during my college years in Shimla, my friends and I would walk 45 mins, sometimes through snow, to the city centre, just to have hot Gulaab Jamuns sold on the roadside by street vendors. When I have a dinner party here this is a set regular sweet which I make time and again since my friends insist on it, as my house is the only place they can get it; after all this is not an item that can be purchased in a bakery down the road, particularly not in Northern Ireland where Indian food is not yet marketed to any scale at all.

Recipe; Makes 25-30 Gulaab Jamuns

Ingredients

3 glasses of dried milk, sieved

1 glass of self raising flour, sieved

4 tablespoons of cooking oil, cold

10 tablespoons of whole creamy milk

Cooking oil for deep frying

Syrup;

5 glasses of sugar

5 glasses of water

3 small green cardamoms split

5-6 cloves

For garnishing;

1 sheet of the vark, the silver paper, and 2-3 pistachios chopped finely

Method

(1) Put the ingredients for the syrup on a medium heat. Bring to the boil and let it simmer for approximately 10-12 mins. Keep it hot.

(2) Meanwhile put the frying oil in a Karaahi or Wok and put it on the cooker to maximum heat. When the oil is hot put the heat off and let the oil cool.

(3) Make the dough; firstly work in the cold oil into the self raising flour with the fingers; then add the milk bit by bit to make a soft dough, which would leave the sides of the bowl and come out clean. At first the dough tends to become sticky when you add the milk, so at this stage use a knife to mix instead of the fingers.

(4) Make small rounds balls, about one inch in diameter and put aside on a greasy surface. This dough should make 25-30 balls.

(5) Put the frying oil on a very low heat and drop the balls in, about 8-10 at a time. Brown them slowly, turning them over constantly. Make each batch the same way.

(6) Take the browned balls out and drain them on a kitchen paper for 2-3 mins. Then drop them in the hot syrup. Do the same with every batch, making sure that those that have absorbed the syrup come on top and the new ones stay dipped in syrup.

(7) Leave them soaking in the syrup for 2-3 hours. Then, move them gently with a slotted spoon into a bowl or a deep tray. They can be served warm by heating them in the microwave; or they can be garnished and served cold. If you are using the silver paper then remember to garnish after warming them in the microwave.

Garnish;

With chopped **pistachios** and a piece of vark, the silver paper (optional)

Serve;

At any time of the day; or as a desert; approximately two per person

Overall cooking time:- 1 to 1 1/2 hours.

Mom's Tips

(1) **A Karaahi or a Wok is the best utensil for this frying** as it allows the balls to be totally immersed in the oil while frying. If using a substitute saucepan make sure there is enough oil in it to do the same.

(2) *I use the creamy top of the whole milk bottles as it seems to have the right proportion of fat and milk.* Otherwise use whole milk not skimmed or toned.

(3) It might seem irrelevant, but **make sure you heat the frying oil** and then cool it down to start frying, because if you only heat it to the required frying temperature then the oil will retain its uncooked taste and flavour which in the end product is not desirable. Remember to keep the heat very low for frying or they will brown on the outside and yet not be properly cooked.

(4) *The round balls of dough will double their original size while frying,* so allow extra room in the oil for expansion. Do not crowd them in the oil as they are soft and gentle and will easily break while turning. Make sure to make smooth balls, with no cracks in them. Also fry them immediately after making them. Do not leave them sitting.

(5) Gulaab jamuns are very good for freezing. Make small portions of 6-8 balls with some syrup in each, and defrost as many portions as required.

(6) **If allergic to nuts omit garnishing**

KULFI, ZAFRANI BADAAM PISTA

(Indian ice-cream with Saffron, Almonds & Pistachios)

A form of traditional Indian ice-cream; **Kulfi is generally made in individual portions and frozen in aluminium cone containers. It looks exquisite when served in its cone shape on the plate and makes for pleasant after dinner conversation** where the guests try and guess how the shape was acquired in the first place. Even though I don't particularly have a sweet tooth; the kulfi remains a firm favourite of mine; comparable to all varieties of ice creams all over the world. My childhood memories are of the summers in Delhi and the street vendors selling these in paper cones with wooden sticks; fascinating for children. Of course the tub variety was also available, small or large, to eat them or take home.

Recipe; Makes 5-7 kulfis

Ingredients

1 litre of whole milk

Pinch of saffron

2 pods of small green cardamoms

2 tablespoons of dried milk

1 tablespoon of cold milk

3-4 tablespoons of sugar

12-15 **almonds** chopped

12-15 **pistachios** chopped

For garnishing;
a few strands of saffron; a vark (optional); **chopped nuts**

Method

(1) Pour the milk into a saucepan and bring it to the boil. Reduce it to simmer Add saffron and the pods of the green cardamom and let it simmer for 25-30 mins or until the milk is reduced to approximately half its quantity

(2) Make a paste of the dried milk with a tablespoon of cold milk and gradually add it to the boiling milk. Let it simmer for another 8-10 mins. Add the sugar to taste. Take off the heat, add the chopped almonds and pistachios and cool the mixture.

(3) Fill the kulfi containers to within 1/2 inch of the top screw them tight and put them in the freezer. Alternatively fill a large ice-cream tub and freeze.

Garnish;
Dip the containers in hot water so that the kulfi can slide out of the containers onto a desert plate, garnish with saffron and vark if available, sprinkle the chopped nuts; serve immediately. If taking our from the larger container then slice the block and serve with garnishing on individual serving

Serve;
as a desert for lunch or dinner; particularly in the summer

Overall cooking time:- 1 hour.

Mom's Tips

(1) Watch the milk when it is coming to the boil as it is easy to spill over; keep an eye on it when simmering for the same reason

(2) A small mini food processor is ideal for chopping the nuts

(3) **Not for those who are allergic to nuts.**

KHEER

(Indian rice pudding);

A very popular North Indian sweet, a favourite of my husband, the origin of this lies in the Hindu religion as Kheer was served at most festivities; infact it still is; but it is also served as an after dinner desert. An all year dish as it can be served hot or cold. Although the description of it is as a rice pudding for obvious reasons, the method of making it and the taste is so different that my Irish friends who would not touch their own rice pudding will have the Indian Kheer any time of the day.

Recipe; Serves 3-4

Ingredients

1 litre of whole milk

2 tablespoons, heaped, of basmati rice

1 small green cardamom, split

5-6 strands of saffron

4 heaped tablespoons of sugar, or according to taste

12-15 kishmish or raisins

6-8 chopped **almonds**

For garnishing;

1 sheet of the vark or the silver paper, 8-10 **almonds** and 12 **pistachios** finely chopped

Method

(1) Soak the saffron strands in two tablespoons of warm milk and set aside.

(2) Wash the rice well, drain in a sieve and set aside.

(3) Put the milk to boil in a broad heavy based pan. Watch the pan; just before the milk comes to the boil put the rice in and stir well. Reduce the heat immediately, before the milk boils again and then let it simmer.

(4) Add the cardamom and the saffron liquid and let the rice and milk cook for about 35-40 mins till it gets a slightly thickish consistency.

(5) Add the sugar, a spoonful at a time and taste it for sweetness as everyone's tastes differ. Add the kishmish, or raisins, and the chopped almonds and let it cook for another 2-3 mins. Take the pan off the heat and let it cool. Stir occasionally to prevent a layer of cream forming on top. At this stage it will have an off white colour with occasional small orangish streaks where the strands of saffron lie. Put in bowls and garnish. Serve warm or cold. It can be warmed in the microwave but remember to garnish after it is warmed.

Garnish;

with *vark first and then sprinkle the chopped almonds and pistachios on top.*

Serve;

Anytime of the day; particularly as a desert.

Overall cooking time:- 1 hour.

Mom's Tips

(1) **Always watch the milk when you set it on the cooker to boil,** as it boils fast and will overflow from the pan very quickly. That is why it is better to use a broad based pan than a deep one. Infact keep a close watch over the pan during the whole cooking for the same reason.

(2) When you take the pan off the heat **leave the kheer thinner than you require** as it will thicken slightly as it cools down. If you feel it has become thicker while it is still on the cooker, add a few spoons of milk and let it boil once before you switch the cooker off. In this case remember to check the sweetness of the pudding again.

(3) You can omit saffron or vark if you are unable to get them, and still enjoy the dish. Also you can increase, decrease, or even omit the raisins or nuts if you do not like them or put in something different like cashew nuts, if you like those.

(4) Not a good dish for freezing, but it will stay in the fridge for 2-3 days.

(5) **If allergic to nuts omit the garnishing with nuts**

SOOJI KA HALVA

(Desert with Semolina);

A North Indian desert, probably the most famous sweet dish possibly of the north and the south as well; enjoyed equally by my 6 years old granddaughter and my 85 years old mother; this is not just a sweet dish made for after dinner; or for a Sunday morning for a special breakfast; it is a dish made on every festive occasion in the house be it a religious occasion or a birthday; it is taken to the temples for religious offerings, it is made in the temples for the parishioners after a 'havan' or a service. **_An interesting dish; easy to make in small or large quantities;_** but it takes practice to achieve that heavenly taste associated with it; yet my twin sons made it for me for a mothers day morning when they were 12 years old, on their own, and very successfully too.

Recipe; Serves 4-6

Ingredients

1 cup of sugar

4 cups of water

3/4 cup melted ghee

1 cup of coarse semolina

15-20 raisins

10-12 **almonds** roughly chopped

For garnishing;

2-3 pods of black cardamoms finely crushed (optional);

8-10 **almonds** crushed or halved.

Method

(1) Put the sugar and the water to boil to make syrup. As soon as it boils take it off the heat and set it aside.

(2) Heat the ghee on a med heat. When hot add the semolina and fry for 10-12 mins or until the semolina is deep brown; the shade of caramel

(3) Reduce the heat and add the syrup and the raisins. Mix well and partially cover; simmer for 3-4 mins or until the water is absorbed. Add the chopped almonds; switch off the heat; cover and leave it sitting on the hot plate for 3-5 mins. Arrange on a shallow plate and serve hot.

Garnish;

sprinkle the crushed pods of cardamoms; arrange the almonds.

Serve;

with breakfast for a special Sunday morning breakfast; or after a meal with ice-cream.

Overall cooking time:- 25-30 mins.

Mom's Tips

(1) Tradionally this dish is made with ghee or butter but it can be substituted for oil, but the taste is definitely better with ghee.

(2) **Measurements are very important** in this recipe as it is easy to spoil the dish

(3) If making in large quantities or for entertaining *make step (1) and (2) the night before and finish off a few minutes before serving.*

(4) **Not a good dish to freeze**, as it does not retain its taste when defrosted.

(5) **If allergic to nuts omit garnishing**

BESAN KI BURFI

(Sweet squares made with Gram flour);

This is a traditional North Indian burfi; the burfi being that group of Indian sweetmeat which can best be described as sweet squares. Generally they have a base of milk solids and the variety is produced by adding different ingredients to the milk solids; almonds, pistachios, cashew nuts even coconut. *The Besan ki Burfi is slightly different as it does not have any milk product in it* and therefore very popular and much in demand in the summer months in India when milk is in short supply and infact most summers, all sweets with milk solids are banned from being sold in the shops. A lovely flavoured sweet square it is easy to make and simple to store.

Recipe; Makes 14-16 squares

Ingredients

1 glass of gram flour

1 glass of sugar, finely ground

3/4 glass of ghee or melted butter

14-16 **almonds** roughly chopped

For garnishing;

1 sheet of vark, the silver sheet(optional), 5-7 **almonds**, roughly chopped

Method

(1) First of all prepare a small 6 or 7 inch square non stick tin which has a removable bottom, lightly oil it and set it aside.

(2) Now heat the ghee in a non stick *karaahi* or a broad based frying pan on a low heat. When hot, add the gram flour and fry it. Keep stirring it all the time and fry on a low heat as the flour is easy to burn, but the flour must get cooked before it browns. This will take about 15-20 mins. when the raw smell of the flour will be replaced by a fried flavour. Take the pan off the heat.

(3) Add the sugar and the chopped almonds, put the pan back on the heat for just 1 min. and mix the sugar in well. Take the pan off the heat. Put the mixture in the prepared cake tin, press it down fairly firmly and smoothen the top.

(4) After about 10-15 mins. while the sweet is still slightly warm, gently take the bottom out of the tin. If you are decorating with a vark slide it now on top of the sweet and then sprinkle the chopped almonds and slightly press them on. Cut the sweet into inch or inch and a half squares, arrange on a flat dish and serve them cold when required. These can be stored in an air-tight jar for 2 weeks.

Garnish;
With vark (silver sheet) and chopped almonds.

Serve;
With coffee at any time of the day, afternoon tea or suppertime.

Overall cooking time:- 35 mins.

Mom's Tips

(1) Ghee gives the best flavour in these squares. Next best would be butter, but ordinary cooking oils do not do justice to this sweet.

(2) The sugar must be ground before adding it or the crunch of the sugar will always be there.

(3) Cut the squares when it is slightly warm; if cold they will crumble slightly.

(4) A good recipe for freezing. Line greaseproof paper in between the squares and then you can take out as many as you require at a time.

(5) **If allergic to nuts omit nuts in the recipe**

ACHAAR AUR CHUTNEY
(Pickles and Chutneys)

Pudeene ki Chutney
(Mint chutney)

Tamaater ki Chutney
(Tomato chutney)

Naariyal-Dahi Chutney
(Coconut chutney with yoghurt)

Gobi, Gaajar, Shalgam ka Achaar
(Cauliflower, Carrot & Turnip pickle)

Meat ka Achaar
(Meat pickle)

Aam ka Achaar
(Mango pickle)

Section 12

India is not a country for preserving fruit or jams; but it is well known for its pickles and chutneys. Interesting accompaniments to an Indian curry, as on the one hand they enhance a set party table, yet on the other, are an excellent addition to a poor man's meal. Tangy and pungent, they are economical to make and serve, as only a small bit on the side of the plate is taken. Because of the number or herbal ingredients in the pickles and chutneys, they are considered to be good for digestion, stimulate appetite and almost essential in the tropics during the hot weather as they are very cooling. **None of these has to be hot, chilli wise,** as commonly assumed, because, if they are being made at home, chillies can be regulated with little problem, and if buying in the supermarkets, watch out for the 'mild' label on most brand names.

The most famous of these is the *mango pickle* or the *'Aam ka Achaar'*. Made of raw, pickling mangoes which, like raspberries, are available only for a fortnight in the month of July, this pickle comes in a variety of forms and tastes. It can be a sweet pickle, a really hot pickle, or made into a chutney. It can be preserved either just with oil, generally mustard oil, or with vinegar or sugar. Depending on the region or the province, the same mango will acquire different taste due to different ingredients. Then there is the *lime pickle* or the *'Nimbu ka achaar'*. This can be made most of the year as limes are generally available. Very popular as it is extremely good for digestion, even stomach cramps. With the correct proportion of salt these pickles will last at least for the year, the lime ones becoming better with the passage of time, sometimes even five years.

Then there is the winter seasonal pickle of *Cauliflower, Carrot and Turnip called 'Gobi, Gaajar and Shalgam ke Achaar'* which will be made in most if not every household in North Western India. It has a crunchy taste; a heavenly pickle

Meat, chicken, pheasant, even partridge pickles are delicious and well known in the North of India although being in the expensive range they are served as delicacies. Not good for long term as they do not preserve as well as the vegetable ones, but then, whenever I have made them they do not last long anyway as my family eats them by the spoonfuls, at any time of the day, with rice, chapaathi or even plain bread.

These pickles, in my young days, were made in earthenware, which were sometimes glazed and often not. This pot was called a **'Bayaam'.** It came in various sizes; the average shape and size of one would have been about twelve inches high, with a round circumference of about eight inches, but it became a short stumped bottleneck on top, leaving it only about three to four inches wide. Now the preserving is done in modern glass jars, but I still think that the taste of the pickles coming out of the Bayaams had a smell of the clay in them which put them in a class of their own.

Basically chutneys serve the same purpose as the pickles that are to add 'oomph' to the meal. In addition, the chutneys are very good with savouries, snacks and tandoori food, same as a dip or a sauce. Samosas and Pakoras taste particularly good with a **Mint chutney** or **Coriander chutney** than with a tomato sauce. Particularly good in the summer when vegetables are in short supply in India. For my twins

birthday parties I do not know what I would have done without Mint, Tomato or Coconut chutneys as I layered the sandwiches with them, and then cut them in an inch wide and three inches long strips which gave the coloured effect of red, yellow and green and yellow in each bite sized sandwich. These never failed to entice the children to eat.

But remember, that whether it is a pickle or chutney, **take a small amount on the plate, one to two spoonfuls, and take a little bit with each morsel of food.** I have seen friends take a whole spoonful at a time like a side vegetable and then spend the evening drinking water or orange juice which defeats the whole purpose of the enjoyment of food.

PUDEENE KI CHUTNEY (Mint chutney);

A very traditional chutney, it is a favourite of the whole country; maybe a bit more so of the north and east, although it is used as an accompaniment for savouries everywhere. ***An easy dish to make as mint is a herb which is used in the east and the west;*** very easy to grow in the garden anywhere, sometimes the problem is to contain its growth. A versatile chutney as it can be varied in its taste by adding yoghurt in it making it more like a dip than a chutney; or adding garlic and ginger making it more like a pickle and serving it with the main meal instead of only with savouries.

Recipe; Makes 1-2 medium jars.

Variation

The most popular variation is;
Add 3 tablespoons of yoghurt to 2 tablespoons of mint chutney;
add 1/4 teaspoon of salt and 1/4 teaspoon of amchur; mix well and serve as a dip with crisps or as a chutney with Pakoras or Seekh Kebabs.

Ingredients

1 bunch of mint, 100gms

1/2 medium sized onion, quartered

1 cooking apple

2-3 small green chillies

1/4 teaspoon of red chillies

1/4 teaspoon of roasted ground jeera

1 teaspoon of dried ground pomegranate or amchur

1 teaspoon of salt

Pinch of sugar

2-3 tablespoons of water

Juice of one lemon

Method

(1) First prepare the mint. If you get a bunch of mint separate the leaves from the stalks and discard the stalks. Wash the leaves well and put them in a liquidizer or a food processor.

(2) Add the onion, cooking apple green chillies, red chillies, ground jeera, pomegranate or amchur, salt, sugar and water. Liquidize it for 1-2 mins.

(3) Add the lemon juice and liquidize again for another 1 min. Check the consistency, which should be like a paste. Taste the salt, it should be just enough with a zing in it; if necessary add a bit more of lemon juice and bottle it.

Preserves;
2-3 weeks in a cool place, preferably the fridge.

Serve;
With any Indian meal, but especially with the chickpea dishes and the meals with pooris in them; Also a necessary accompaniment with any Indian snack or savoury.

Overall making time:- 1/2 hr.

Mom's Tips

(1) I prefer to use a liquidizer instead of a food processor as it seems to make a better paste; the food processor seems to chop everything finely but does not integrate it into the water and lemon juice as well as a liquidizer does.

(2) Although the ground pomegranate seeds or the amchur adds to the lovely tangy taste but if you are not able to get them, omit them and add another spoon of lemon juice to the chutney.

(3) A good chutney to freeze in small batches. Consume within 3-4 days of defrosting

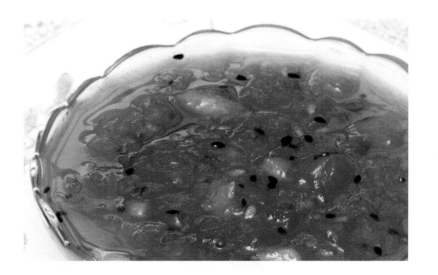

TAMAATER KI CHUTNEY

(Tomato chutney);

A modern chutney, it incorporates spices of the north and south. Very well **flavoured, but mild, it is equally nice as an accompaniment with Indian food or with western, particularly with the cold meats.** Of course, if you prefer it hot you can increase the proportion of the red chillies, even of the garam masaala in the recipe. Remember to get the edible onion seeds for this recipe instead of the flowering ones; it was a discussion that I always had with the girls in my cooking classes when we reached this particular recipe.

Recipe; Make 2-4 jars depending on the size of the jars.

Ingredients

1 kg of red soft tomatoes

1 cup of sugar

3/4 cup of malt vinegar

1/4 cup of lemon juice

3-4 cloves of garlic, finely chopped

1 inch cube of ginger, finely chopped

1/2 teaspoon of red chillies

1/2 teaspoon of garam masaala

1 teaspoon of salt

Tarka; (Garnish)

2 green chillies, quartered (optional)

1 teaspoon of methre seeds

1 teaspoon of whole jeera

1 teaspoon of black mustard seeds

1 teaspoon of onion seeds

2 tablespoons of mustard oil

Method

(1) First prepare the tomatoes. Put the tomatoes in boiling water for 2-3 mins. or until the skins burst. Take the skins off the tomatoes, chop the tomatoes and put them in a saucepan.

(2) Add the sugar, vinegar and lemon juice and bring to the boil. Add the garlic, ginger, red chillies, garam masaala and salt.

(3) Lower the heat and simmer for 45 mins to 1 hour or until the chutney is thickish, **something like the consistency of jam or marmalade when it is taken off the heat.** Do not let it be the right consistency as it will thicken as it cools. Take it off the heat and leave it to cool.

(4) Heat the oil in a heavy based frying pan on a high heat. Heat the oil until you see the smoke rising off the oil and it may even sting your eyes. Take it off the heat, add the quartered green chillies and the whole spices and fry for 10 secs. Pour this tarka over the chutney and mix well. Cool it completely before bottling the chutney. Keep it in the fridge or in a cool place and it should stay for at least a month.

Preserves:-

1-2 months in the fridge or a cool place.

Serve;

With any Indian meal; or a western meal, particularly a cold salad or to accompany cold meats; or with a snack or savoury instead of tomato sauce.

Overall cooking time:- 1 1/2 hrs.

Mom's Tips

(1) **It is important to make sure the tomatoes are soft and red,** infact your green grocer will be glad to sell a day old tomatoes at a reduced price as mine is. So take advantage of it. Sometimes tomatoes are more juicy and sometimes less, so regulate the boiling time accordingly.

(2) **Remember to totally smoke the oil otherwise,** as I have said elsewhere, mustard oil has a very pungent taste which it loses in the burning. So watch the oil when heating, do not leave it unattended.

(3) The chutney will keep for a month or two; it may keep longer, but I have never had the occasion to find out as mine at home is eaten long before its expiry time

NARRIYAL-DAHI CHUTNEY

(Coconut chutney with yoghurt);

A **well known and extremely popular chutney of the South of India; a basic and integral accompaniment of the most well known dishes of this region;** Idli, Sambhar, vada; none of which would be served without this chutney or its variations. An unusual chutney as the basic ingredients, coconut and yoghurt are not tangy foods; it needs the addition of lemon juice, in some variations even tamarind, to give it the tangy and sour taste of the chutneys. My sons loved it with any group of foods, even snacks. It makes an interesting variation at any time of the day; I have served it before a meal as a dip; I have set it on the table as chutney when we are entertaining.

Recipe; makes 2 medium sized containers.

Ingredients

1/2 fresh coconut kernel

3 cloves of garlic

2 inch cube ginger

1-2 green chilli

3 tablespoons of chopped coriander

1/2 teaspoon garam masaala

2-3 tablespoon water

2 tablespoons lemon juice

2 cups of natural yoghurt

1 teaspoon salt

Tarka; (Garnish)

2 tablespoons of oil

1 Tablespoons of washed urad daal or channa daal

2 red chillies whole

6-7 kari pattas

2 teaspoons black mustard seeds

2 teaspoons ground fenugreek

1/2 teaspoon red chillies or paprika

Method

(1) Cut the coconut into small pieces and put them in a food processor along with the garlic, ginger, chillies and coriander and process with 2-3 tablespoon of water and the two tablespoons of lemon juice till it becomes a coarse paste.

(2) Add the yoghurt, salt and garam masaala, mix well and set aside.

It should be the consistency of a coarse batter.

(3) Wash the daal and soak for 10 mins. Drain and set aside. Heat the oil in a shallow frying pan. Add the red chillies whole and the kari patta and fry for 20 secs. Add the daal and fry on a low heat for 3-4 mins or until golden brown. Take out in a small dish.

(4) Add the mustard seeds of the pan and sizzle them for 30 secs. Add the daal mixture, the ground fenugreek and the red chillies and fry for 30 secs. Pour over the coconut and yoghurt mixture and mix. Serve cold.

Serve;

With any Indian meal; particularly any south Indian food, uttapam, dosa, idli, rice and sambhar, vada and sambhar or any snack

Overall cooking time:- 1/2 hr.

Mom's Tips

(1) This chutney does not freeze well. It also does not keep for more than 2-3 days in the fridge; but the coarse paste can be frozen in small batches after step 1 and taken as required and finished with step (2), (3)and (4) before serving.

GOBI, GAAJAR, SHALGAM KA ACHAAR
(Cauliflower, Carrot & Turnip pickle)

This pickle is as popular in the Panjab as fish in Bengal or Tamarind in Delhi or coconut in Kerala. In the ***villages of the Panjab a whole meal can consist of chapaathi, home made butter and this pickle;*** and as it has the three most favoured vegetables there is something for all tastes. It can only be made in the winter as these are the vegetables of the season and will preserve only for the winter three to four months as the onset of heat will spoil it. **An interesting pickle as it can be made very spicy; very sweet; with uncooked vegetables or with blanched vegetables.** I have written the recipe for the one I favoured the most; a mild pickle, easy for children and adults alike; and for this reason also the one that finished the quickest.

Recipe; for 2-3 medium sized jars, depending on the size

Ingredients

1 1/2 kg cauliflower, washed, cut into bite sized pieces

1 1/2 kg carrots, peeled, washed, cur into bite size pieces

1 1/2 kg of turnip, peeled, washed, cut into bite size pieces

3-4 onions, finely chopped; optional

4 pieces of ginger, 1 inch cubes, finely chopped

20-25 cloves of garlic, finely chopped

8-10 cloves

3 sticks of cinnamon, each stick 1 inch long

4 black cardomoms, deseeded

1 inch stick of ratanjot, optional

2 tablespoons of ground cumin

1 tablespoon of red chillies

2 tablespoons of salt

4 tablespoons of rai pickling seeds

1 kg of sugar

3/4 litre of malt vinegar

6-7 tablespoons of mustard oil

Method

(1) Mix the cut vegetables, put them into boiling water and drain them immediately. Spread them flat in on a sheet and let them dry thoroughly.

(2) Heat the mustard oil. When it is so hot that it smokes then take it off the heat. Add the cloves, cinnamon and cardamoms; put the oil back on heat; add the onion, garlic, ginger; fry for 4-5 mins or until golden brown. Add the ratanjot for the colour. Switch off the heat.

(3) Add the rest of the spices, cumin chilli, salt and the pickling rai seed; also add the sugar and mix well.

(4) Add the vegetables and mix. Add the vinegar; mix thoroughly and leave to cool for 6-8 hours. Then bottle the pickle.

Preserves;
2-3 months in a cool place

Serve;
with any Indian meal; on a slice of bread as a snack.

Overall cooking time;- 40 mins for preparation and 40 mins for cooking and making the pickle.

Mom's Tips

(1) **Make sure the vegetable pieces are really dry** before putting them in the oil mixture or the pickle will not preserve well. Sometimes it can take up to 12 hours to dry them properly.

(2 *The weight of the vegetables* given in this recipe is after the vegs have been prepared; in this recipe this is important as it is in proportion to the sugar, salt and vinegar for the preserving process.

(3) *The small white turnips that come in the summer have a better taste* in this pickle probably because these are like the turnips that we get in India.

(4) **The heating of the mustard oil is to the point of the oil smoking. is important** otherwise it will taste of mustard which is not the right taste for pickle.

MEAT KA ACHAAR

(Meat Pickle)

A North Indian speciality, **this is a pickle generally available in the colder regions of the north,** starting from the foothills of the Himalayas where is easier to preserve it. *For the same reason it is more popular in the winter than in the summer, and also the intake of meat reduces in the hot weather anyway.* When I was first married I went to live in Chandigarh, in the Panjab, from where the foothills of the mountains are just thirty miles away. Many a winter afternoon saw my husband and me go up to the mountains on our motorbike just to collect this pickle which was made and sold by a couple just on the main highway between Chandigarh and Shimla. The wait in the queue was as long as our journey took but then the pickle we got was more than worth it.

Recipe; 2-3 pickling jars, depending on the size of the jars.

Ingredients

1kg of lamb meat, preferably the leg, boned

2 teaspoons of salt

1 teaspoon of garam masaala

750 ml. malt vinegar

2 tablespoons of sugar

2 medium sized bulbs of garlic, peeled

2 inch cube of ginger

1 piece of 2 inches long cinnamon

1 tablespoon of red chillies

2 tablespoons of pickling rai, finely ground

1 glass of water

250 ml mustard oil

Method

(1) First prepare the garlic and ginger. Cut them into long thin strips, the garlic can be the whole of its length, and the ginger can be as long as the garlic, about half an inch long. Set them aside.

(2) Put the vinegar and sugar on to boil. Let it boil for about 10-12 mins, or until the quantity reduces to 1/4

(3) Then prepare the meat. Trim the fat off the meat completely and dice the meat into small 1/2 inch cubed pieces and put into a heavy based pan. Put in 1 glass of water, 1 teaspoon of garam masaala and 1 teaspoon of salt. Bring it to the boil, lower the heat and simmer it for 25-30 mins to tenderize the meat. Then dry it completely and take it off the heat.

(4) Now heat the mustard oil in a heavy based pan on a high heat till you see the smoke rising from the pan. It could also sting your eyes but it is harmless. Take it off the heat and add the piece of cinnamon, garlic and ginger and put it back on a low heat. Fry for 1 min. or until the garlic and ginger is golden brown. Take it off the heat and mix in the red chillies.

(5) Add the cooked but dry meat to the above oil mixture, mix well and put it back on the heat. Fry for 5-6 mins, mixing constantly. Then take it off the heat and add the rai. Mix well again. Slowly add the vinegar and sugar mixture, stirring all the time. Set it aside to cool. Keep mixing it every hour or so while it is cooling. It should be completely cold before you bottle it.

Preserves:-
3-4 weeks. Keep in a cool place but not in the fridge as the meat tastes better if at room temperature.

Serve;
With any Indian meal; or with a western meal of a cold salad; also as a snack as it can be had with plain white or brown bread.

Overall cooking time:- 1 hour 15 mins.

Mom's Tips

(1) Make sure that there is no fat left on the meat as you trim and prepare the meat. Also make sure the meat is completely dry before putting it in the oil as any water or juices left will tend to counteract the preservatives.

(2) **The mustard oil must be smoked** before you put anything in it or it will have a very pungent taste and smell, which disappears in the smoke.

(3) *The garlic and ginger must be browned* or the pickle will have raw garlicky taste and smell.

(4) **Red chillies and rai must be added after taking the oil** off the heat and letting it sit for 1-2 mins, as they burn easily and will lose their colour.

AAM KA ACHAAR

(Mango pickle)

This is a very traditional pickle, probably the only pickle in India which is made in different provinces with different variations. Therefore there is the Panjabi mango pickle which is different from the Hyderabadi one, which again is different to the Gujarati pickle. Each one has a different combination of spices; some have them cooked, some uncooked. Some varieties are cooked with mustard oil, some with ordinary cooking oil and some without oil. *This is not to be confused with the mango chutney which is totally different in style, taste and texture Here is the recipe for the Panjabi pickle which is probably the most well known of all its variations.*

The pickling mango is available only for a fortnight in July in India. In my childhood this pickle was always made in the large **pickling clay pots called 'Bayaams'** which gave it a lovely mature taste; but then my mother and grandmother also had years of experience in making this to perfection. *Easy to make but, like all pickles the 'oomph' in it needs practice.*

Recipe; Makes 3 medium sized glass jars, depending on the size or 1 large clay pickling pot.

Ingredients

5 kg raw pickling mangoes

200 gms fennel seeds

200 gms fenugreek seeds

100 gms black pepper

100 gms turmeric

100 gms red chillies, ground

100 gms kalongi (onion seeds)

1 kg salt

100 gms whole red chillies (optional)

1 litre mustard oil

Method

(1) Wash and cut the mangoes into small pieces with the seed. Set aside.

(2) Grind the aniseed, fenugreek and black pepper coarsely and set aside. Mix turmeric, red chillies and onion seeds and mix them well in the oil. Then add the coarsely ground spices and mix them again.

(3) Put the Mango pieces in the clay pot or a large container and mix half of the spice and oil mixture well. Cover and set aside.

(4) Next day add the other half of the spice mixture and mix. Add the whole red chillies also and mix. Cover and set aside in a warm sunny place for 10-12 days. Mix the pickle well once a day. Then put it into the jars.

Preserves;

1-2 years

Serve;

With any Indian meal or with a snack or savouries.

Overall cooking time;

1 hr for preparation; 10 mins for making it.

Mom's Tips

(1) *Make sure that the utensils are dry* when making this pickle as a touch of water would spoil it and it will not last.

(2) **The weight of the vegetables in proportion to the salt and the oil is particularly important for preserving the pickle.** The red chillies can be increased or decreased according to taste.

(3) *The onion seeds must not be ground* with the aniseed, fenugreek and the black pepper or the taste will alter.

DIVAALI;

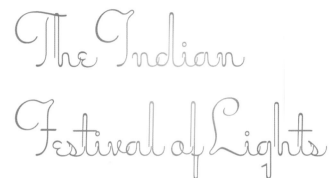

The Indian Festival of Lights

& more

Divaali is the most important festival of the Hindus. With its origin in the mythology of the Hindu religion, **it encompasses the entire society and, as with Christmas in Britain, or even Thanksgiving in America,** *it provides the focal event for families to gather, friends to meet, feuds to heal and children to merry make.* **It is the day that new beginnings are made; if someone's has built a new house, they move in on Divaali day; if a new business is to start, the day of Divaali is the day to start it on; it is the day for which spring cleaning is done, houses are painted, decorations are put up, festivities are organised.**

Last year Divaali was on the 9th of November. It is not the date on which it is every year. Rather, like Easter, the date changes every year. The reason is that the Indian calendar is a lunar calendar and works by the moon cycle of 32 days, as opposed to the western calendar of 30-31 days per month. So in the beginning of every year the Indian Pundits work out the dates of the Indian festivals and by that permutation combination, this year Divaali was in the middle of November; on the night of no moon or 'Amavasya'.

The reason for it being on the darkest night of the month is important and part of the story of Divaali. According to the mythology of 'Ramayana', one of our holy books, Lord Rama, who is believed to be the seventh reincarnation of Lord Vishnu who came to the earth to fight evil and show the path of righteousness to the people, had in the course of his trials and tribulations, suffered fourteen years in exile with his wife Sita and younger brother Lakshman, from his kingdom of *'Avadh'* in the north of India. The culmination of these years was his victory over Raavana, the ruler of Sri Lanka (Ceylon), with the help of Hanuman, the monkey God who represents total devotion. Raavana symbolizes the forces of evil and his

This then is the spirit of Divaali. On this night, as a token of the safe return of Lord Rama to his rightful place, **the whole of India illuminates.** Every house, every street, every shop, even the government buildings, all light Diyas on their window sills, walls and roof tops. When we were children I remember our father bringing home hundreds of Diyas in cartons, and we used to spend weeks making cotton wicks for them and filling them with oil. We also had a couple of beautiful brass Diyas which we would polish till they shone; place them on the bay window, from where the flame would reflect through the dozen panes of glass. Now of course life has moved on, nobody has the time, anyway modernization has come in and wax candles have replaced the Diyas; they give the same light, perhaps not the same spirit. Here in Northern Ireland, more often than not, the wind and the rain make it difficult for the candles to be lit outside; so most of us light them inside the house as a token.

Firecrackers are the rage of the day; from the simple sparklers to the boomers and the rockets in the sky, the range is enormous, with new ones added every year. If there has been a wedding or a birth in the family in that year the celebrations can go on till the early hours of the morning! As Halloween and Guy Falkes night in Britain are at the same time of the year, fire crackers here are very easy to obtain, although because of restrictions on their operation, sometimes we have had to do with sparklers only.

The sweetmeat shops open twenty - four hours a day for the whole week; infact it is said that if a new sweetmeat businesses to start it should be at Divaali as it will recoup its entire setting up costs before the week is up. Gold and jewellery shops have their biggest turnover in this month. Premieres of new movies are scheduled for Divaali night; more often than not two will be slated as 'Om Shanti Om' and 'Saawariya', the two hyped up movies for 2007 were, and their

defeat is celebrated as 'Dusshehra' in Northwest India and as 'Durga-puja, in Northeast India as the victory of good over evil. This is linked to the Divaali celebrations as it always comes twenty days before Divaali. The night Lord Rama returned from his fourteen years of wanderings it was a totally dark night, no moon, and because the people of his capital *'Ayodhya'* wanted to celebrate his return, as he was their rightful ruler, they lit the city with Indian style candles, which traditionally are wicks burnt in mustard oil in little earthen pots called *'Diyas'.* They painted the sky red with firecrackers to illuminate his path, distributed sweetmeats to the poor and made merry for days.

&more

endless controversies and arguments carried on for weeks before and after.

With new clothes, exchange of presents and a new item for the house, be it household or furniture, which is tradition, the day moves on to noisy family gatherings, lighting up of the candles, deafening crackers and rich food; and closes in the evening, around midnight, with half an hour of traditional prayers in each house itself

Divaali celebrations cannot end without a mention of this 'Lakshmi puja', which means praying to Lakshmi, the goddess of wealth. Lakshmi is the consort of Lord Vishnu, whose reincarnation is Lord Rama; and possibly it is the reason for this ritual as people do believe that this will bring them wealth and prosperity in the coming year. This is part of my childhood memories in which my father always performed this puja on Divaali evening and is an integral part of the celebrations which come to a close with 'Bhai Dooj' an occasion and a ritual between brothers and sisters and is always on the third day after Divaali. In this the sisters apply a 'tikka' or a red

mark on the brother's forehead and pray for his long life and get gifts and blessings in return. Possibly in the past it was set in as part of the celebration to give the married girls an opportunity, sanctioned by society and religion, to visit their own parent's homes as well during this auspicious time.

An exhausting but fulfilling festival, takes half a year to plan for and half a year to recover from it financially. Did someone say it reminded them of Christmas? That is why I said the words at the start; it is comparable to Christmas in Britain, Thanksgiving in America; a time steeped in ritual and tradition, a time for fun and laughter.

notes

notes